T H E   B O O K   O F
Cheesecakes

THE BOOK OF

Cheesecakes

STEVEN WHEELER

Photography by
PAUL GRATER

a Salamander book
Published by Salamander Books Limited
LONDON • NEW YORK

Published 1988 by Salamander Books Ltd,
52 Bedford Row, London WC1R 4LR
By arrangement with Merehurst Press,
5 Great James Street, London WC1N 3DA

© Copyright Merehurst Limited 1988

ISBN 0 86101 283 6

Managing Editor: Felicity Jackson
Designer: Roger Daniels
Home Economist: Steven Wheeler
Photographer: Paul Grater
Typeset by AKM Associates (UK) Ltd, Southall, London
Colour separation by J. Film Process Ltd, Bangkok, Thailand.
Printed by New Interlitho S.p.A., Milan

ACKNOWLEDGEMENTS

The Publishers would like to thank the following for their
help and advice:
June Budgen
David Mellor of 26 James Street, Covent Garden,
London WC2E 8PA, 4 Sloane Square, London SW1W 8EE
and 66 King Street, Manchester M2 4NP
Philips Home Appliances, City House, 420-430 London Road,
Croydon CR9 3QR
Prestige Master Baker kindly supplied by Prestige Group U.K. PLC,
14-18 Holborn, London EC1 2LQ

Companion volumes of interest:
The book of COCKTAILS
The book of CHOCOLATES & PETITS FOURS
The book of HORS D'OEUVRES
The book of GARNISHES
The book of PRESERVES
The book of SAUCES
The book of ICE CREAMS & SORBETS
The book of GIFTS FROM THE PANTRY
The book of PASTA
The book of HOT & SPICY NIBBLES – DIPS – DISHES
The book of CRÊPES & OMELETTES
The book of FONDUES
The book of BISCUITS

CONTENTS

INTRODUCTION

Sinfully delicious, cheesecakes are guaranteed to win favour with all guests, young and old. Hosts and hostesses have been known to earn their entire culinary reputation from the success of one cheesecake, and no other dessert invokes so much talk about secret ingredients, special bases and toppings.

The Book of Cheesecakes is a collection of a hundred fantastic recipes for this most luxurious of treats. It includes my personal versions of classics such as the Russian Easter cheesecake, Paskha, and New York's favourite, Lindy's Cheesecake, as well as a whole range of others, including fruit cheesecakes, chocolate cheesecakes, ones made with spices, wine or spirits, low fat ones and individual cheesecakes.

Many are suitable for lunch and dinner parties, others can be enjoyed at tea or coffee time. Also included are a number of savoury cheesecakes which make deliciously different starters or main courses.

Every recipe is photographed in full colour and there are step-by-step instructions for making unusual sponge borders, both plain and chocolate, and special cheesecake pastries which make a firm base for the rich creamy fillings.

The Book of Cheesecakes will enable you to entertain in style, producing elegant desserts with the minimum of fuss and effort.

EQUIPMENT

The great advantage of a cheesecake is the ease with which it can be put together. All the cheesecakes in this book have been prepared using the minimum of equipment.

Wooden spoon and mixing bowl Most of the cheesecake fillings are simple mixtures of cheese, cream and eggs beaten together in a bowl with a wooden spoon, then turned onto a pastry or biscuit crumb base.

Food processor A food processor can be used for mixing the fillings, and will give a very light texture.

Loose-bottomed tins The tin for a cheesecake is important as most have to be removed from the tin the right way up. Loose-bottomed tins, which simply lift out from the sides, are ideal. They come in various sizes, both square and round, the most useful being 20 cm (8 in) and 22.5 cm (9 in). Line the base to prevent sticking.

Spring-form tins These tins are particularly good for larger cheesecakes. As well as the loose base, they have a spring clip which releases the sides, allowing the cheesecake to be removed without any risk of damaging the sides.

Terrines These can be used to give a different shaped cheesecake, but are only suitable for ones that are inverted to turn out.

Baking sheets and tartlet moulds Baking sheets are needed for roulades. Tartlet moulds are used to make individual cheesecakes.

Other shapes The traditional mould for Paskha is a flower pot and for Coeurs à la Crème, special heart-shaped moulds are needed.

Piping bag and nozzles These are used for piping out the fancy sponge borders before baking and also for piping cream to decorate.

CHEESES

All the sweet cheesecakes in this book are made with soft cheeses. These are spreadable cheeses, most of which do not keep for very long and should be bought in small quantities when you want to use them. The cheeses may be lumpy with curds, smooth and creamy, or moulded into firm blocks. Some of the savoury cheesecakes use other, stronger-flavoured cheeses such as Gruyère, Parmesan or goat's cheese.

The fat content of soft cheeses varies considerably and the terms low fat, medium fat and so on are a guide only. In most recipes the cheeses are interchangeable, the only difference will be in texture.

Low fat cheese This contains between 2 and 10% fat and produces a light cheesecake.

Cottage cheese This may have a very low or medium fat content depending on what has been added to it. It has large soft curds and needs beating or sieving before using in a cheesecake.

Ricotta cheese Italian Ricotta cheese is traditionally made from whey rather than curds, but Ricotta may have full or skimmed milk added to it, so fat content varies from low to medium.

Medium fat soft cheese This contains between 10 and 20% fat. Medium fat curd cheese can be substituted in any recipe calling for medium fat soft cheese.

Full fat soft cheese This is a general name given to soft cheeses with a minimum of 20% fat. However, the fat content can be 60% or over and when a recipe calls for full fat soft cheese this is the sort that should be used.

Mascarpone This cheese looks like a thick velvety cream, but is sweeter. It has a fat content of 45–55%.

── PLAIN SPONGE BORDER ──

3 eggs at room temperature
9 teaspoons caster sugar
30 g (1 oz/¼ cup) plain flour

Preheat oven to 220C (425F/Gas 7). Line a large baking sheet with greaseproof paper. Using a rotary or hand-held whisk, beat eggs and sugar in a bowl until mixture is thick enough to hold trail of the whisk when beaters are lifted.

Sift flour over egg mixture and fold in carefully with a large metal spoon. Immediately, spoon mixture into a piping bag fitted with a 1 cm (½ in) nozzle. Using minimal pressure, pipe out as many lines as possible across narrow side of the baking sheet, so that they just touch each other. Bake in the top of the oven for 10–12 minutes or until springy to the touch.

Turn out onto a clean tea towel so that lining paper is uppermost. Leave to cool. When cool, cut into strips measuring the depth of cheese-cake tin. Leave the paper on until ready to use.

Sufficient for lining a 22.5 cm (9 in) tin.

Note: The sponge border can be fitted in 2 pieces around the inside of the cake tin.

– CHOCOLATE SPONGE BORDER –

3 eggs at room temperature
9 teaspoons caster sugar
30 g (1 oz/¼ cup) plain flour
3 teaspoons cocoa powder

Preheat oven to 220C (425F/Gas 7). Line a large baking sheet with greaseproof paper. Using a rotary or hand-held whisk, beat eggs and sugar in a bowl until mixture is thick enough to hold trail of the whisk when beaters are lifted.

Divide mixture between 2 smaller bowls. Sift 6 teaspoons flour over one of the bowls and fold in carefully with a large metal spoon. Immediately, spoon mixture into a piping bag fitted with a 1 cm (½ in) nozzle. Using minimal pressure, pipe out as many lines as possible across narrow side of the baking sheet, one finger's width apart.

Sift remaining flour and the cocoa powder over second bowl and fold in. Spoon into piping bag and pipe between the lines. Bake in top of oven for 10–12 minutes or until springy to touch. Turn out onto a tea towel to cool, leaving grease-proof paper on top. When cool, cut into 5–7.5 cm (2–3 in) strips, depending on depth of tin.

Sufficient for lining a 22.5 cm (9 in) tin.

CHEESECAKE PASTRY

125 g (4 oz/1 cup) plain flour
90 g (3 oz/¾ cup) self-raising flour
60 g (2 oz/¼ cup) caster sugar
125 g (4 oz/½ cup) cool salted butter, cut into pieces
2 egg yolks

Sift flours into a large bowl or food processor. Stir in the sugar.

Add butter and rub in with finger tips until mixture resembles large breadcrumbs, or blend in a food processor for 1 minute.

Add egg yolks and mix to a smooth dough. If pastry feels very soft, leave in the refrigerator to allow butter to firm, otherwise pastry can be rolled out straight away.

Sufficient for lining a 22.5 cm (9 in) tin or dish.

Note: The pastry can be kept in the refrigerator for up to 4 days. Allow to soften at room temperature before using.

—SWEET SHORTCRUST PASTRY —

250 g (8 oz/2 cups) plain flour
6 teaspoons icing sugar
125 g (4 oz/½ cup) cool butter or margarine, cut into pieces
1 egg, beaten
few drops vanilla essence

Sift flour and icing sugar into a large bowl or food processor.

Add butter or margarine and rub in with fingertips until mixture resembles breadcrumbs, or blend in a food processor for about 45 seconds.

Add beaten egg and essence and mix to a smooth dough. Wrap in plastic wrap and leave in the refrigerator for 1 hour before rolling out.

Sufficient for lining a 20 cm (8 in) tin or dish.

Note: This pastry can be kept in the refrigerator for up to 4 days, or it can be frozen for up to 6 weeks.

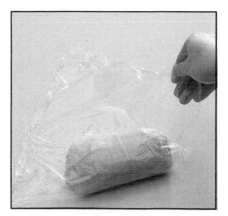

——AMARETTI CHEESECAKE——

60 g (2 oz/¼ cup) butter
60 g (2 oz/½ cup) sweetmeal biscuit crumbs
90 g (3 oz) macaroons, broken into pieces
FILLING:
500 g (1 lb) medium fat soft cheese
155 ml (5 fl oz/⅔ cup) thick sour cream
90 g (3 oz/⅓ cup) caster sugar
3 eggs, separated
3 teaspoons plain flour
few drops almond essence
finely grated peel and juice of 1 lemon
TO DECORATE:
440 g (14 oz) can apricot halves
155 ml (5 fl oz/⅔ cup) whipping cream

Grease and line a 22.5 cm (9 in) round, loose-bottomed cake tin. In a saucepan, melt butter, then stir in biscuit crumbs and macaroons. Mix well, then press into base of tin.

In a bowl, beat cheese, sour cream and 60 g (2 oz/¼ cup) sugar. Add egg yolks, flour and almond essence, then stir in lemon peel and juice. Mix well.

Whisk egg whites with remaining sugar in a bowl, then fold into cheese mixture, using a large metal spoon. Turn into cake tin and leave to set in the refrigerator for 2–3 hours, or until firm.

To decorate, drain apricot halves on absorbent kitchen paper, then arrange them over the top of the cheesecake. In a bowl, whip cream until stiff, then pipe rosettes of cream in between each of the apricot halves. Chill thoroughly before serving.

Serves 12.

— BLACK FOREST CHEESECAKE —

90 g (3 oz/⅓ cup) butter	
185 g (6 oz/1⅔ cups) chocolate biscuit crumbs	
FILLING:	
750 g (1½ lb) full fat soft cheese	
3 eggs	
125 g (4 oz/½ cup) caster sugar	
220 g (7 oz) can black cherries	
6 teaspoons cocoa powder	
1 teaspoon ground cinnamon	
90 ml (3 fl oz/⅓ cup) whipping cream	
125 g (4 oz) plain (dark) chocolate, broken into pieces	
TOPPING:	
440 g (14 oz) can black cherries	
4 teaspoons cornflour	

Preheat oven to 180C (350F/Gas 4). Grease and line a 20 cm (8 in) round, loose-bottomed cake tin. In a saucepan, melt butter, then stir in biscuit crumbs. Mix well, then press into base of cake tin.

In a bowl, beat cheese, eggs and sugar. Spread half the mixture onto biscuit base. Drain cherries and arrange them over cheese mixture.

Stir cocoa powder and cinnamon into remaining cheese mixture. In a small saucepan, bring cream to the boil. Add chocolate and remove from heat while chocolate melts. Leave to cool, then mix into cheese mixture. Pour into cake tin, then bake in the oven for 45 minutes. Leave to cool in the tin.

To decorate, leave cheesecake in the tin. Drain cherry juice from 440 g (14 oz) can cherries into a saucepan and bring to boil. Mix cornflour with 2 tablespoons water, stir into cherry juice and simmer to thicken. When thick, add cherries and arrange on top of cheesecake. Leave until topping is firm before removing from tin.

Serves 8–10.

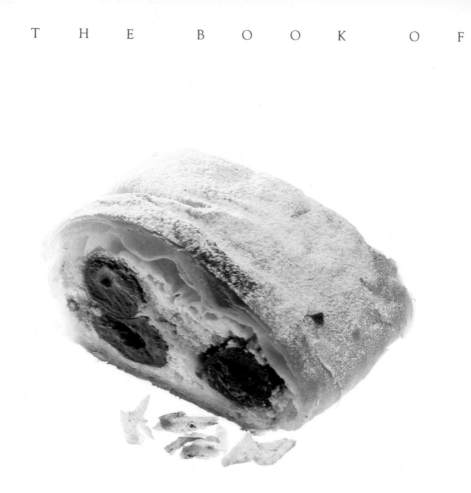

CHERRY CHEESE STRUDEL

185 g (6 oz) Ricotta cheese
125 g (4 oz) cottage cheese
60 ml (2 fl oz/¼ cup) thick sour cream
3 tablespoons ground almonds
220 g (7 oz/1 cup) butter
125 g (4 oz/2 cups) fresh breadcrumbs
8 sheets filo pastry
375 g (12 oz) can black cherries
90 g (3 oz/⅓ cup) dark soft brown sugar
TO SERVE:
icing sugar
single (light) cream

Preheat oven to 200C (400F/Gas 6). In a bowl, beat cheeses and sour cream. Stir in almonds. In a large frying pan, melt 90 g (3 oz/⅓ cup) of the butter and fry breadcrumbs until golden.

Spread a clean tea towel on a table and dust with flour. Melt remaining butter in a saucepan. Place sheet of pastry on tea towel and brush with melted butter. Cover with a second sheet of pastry and continue until pastry and most of the butter are used up. Spread cheese mixture over two-thirds of the pastry.

Drain cherries and arrange on cheese. Sprinkle fried breadcrumbs and brown sugar over cherries. Using the tea towel, roll up filling and pastry into a long sausage. Brush pastry with remaining melted butter. Bake in the oven for 40 minutes until golden. Dust with icing sugar and serve with cream.

Serves 8.

— CONTINENTAL CHEESECAKE —

1 quantity Sweet Shortcrust Pastry, see page 13

FILLING:

500 g (1 lb) cottage cheese

155 ml (5 fl oz/⅔ cup) whipping cream

3 eggs, separated

90 g (3 oz/⅓ cup) caster sugar

60 g (2 oz/½ cup) ground almonds

finely grated peel and juice of 1 lemon

60 g (2 oz/⅓ cup) mixed citrus peel

60 g (2 oz/⅓ cup) sultanas

TO GLAZE:

1 egg yolk

¼ teaspoon salt

Preheat oven to 190C (375F/Gas 5). Lightly grease a 20 x 25 cm (8 x 10 in), 4 cm (1½ in) deep, baking tin. Roll out pastry on a lightly floured surface to a thickness of 0.5 cm (¼ in) and line base and sides of tin. Reserve trimmings. Fill tin with dried beans or pasta and bake in the oven for 20 minutes. Remove beans and set aside pastry case. Lower oven temperature to 180C (350F/Gas 4).

To make filling, beat cheese, cream and egg yolks in a bowl. Add 60 g (2 oz/¼ cup) sugar, the ground almonds, lemon peel and juice and beat until smooth. Stir in mixed citrus peel and sultanas.

Whisk the egg whites in a bowl with remaining 30 g (1 oz/5 teaspoons) caster sugar until firm. Fold beaten egg into cheese mixture with a large metal spoon.

Roll out reserved pastry trimmings and cut into strips. Use to decorate top of cheesecake. Mix together egg yolk and salt for the glaze and brush over pastry strips. Bake in the oven for 40 minutes.

Leave to cool, then cut into fingers to serve.

Serves 10–12.

KASTOBERSTORTE

4 eggs
9 teaspoons caster sugar
6 teaspoons plain flour
6 teaspoons cornflour
250 g (8 oz) medium fat curd cheese
155 ml (5 fl oz/⅔ cup) natural yogurt
60 g (2 oz/⅓ cup) raisins
finely grated peel and juice of 1 orange
155 ml (5 fl oz/⅔ cup) whipping cream
3 teaspoons powdered gelatine
6 teaspoons clear honey
icing sugar for dusting

Preheat oven to 200C (400F/Gas 6). Lightly grease 2 baking sheets and line with non-stick baking parchment. Mark two 22.5 cm (9 in) circles on baking parchment.

Using a rotary or hand-held whisk, beat 2 eggs and the sugar in a bowl until mixture is thick enough to hold trail of whisk when beaters are lifted. Sift flours over eggs and fold in with a large metal spoon.

Spoon mixture onto baking sheets, spreading it beyond circles. Bake in the oven for 12–15 minutes with oven door open 1 cm (½ in).

Meanwhile, make filling, blend cheese, yogurt, raisins and orange peel and juice in a bowl. Whip cream and fold in. Sprinkle gelatine over 2 tablespoons water in a small bowl and leave to soften for 2–3 minutes. Stand bowl in a saucepan of hot water and stir until dissolved and quite hot. Stir into cheese. Beat remaining eggs and honey until thick, then fold into cheese.

Using a sharp knife, trim sponges to 22.5 cm (9 in) diameter. Fit one sponge into a 22.5 cm (9 in) loose-bottomed cake tin. Pour filling on top and refrigerate for 2–3 hours until set. Place second sponge on filling and dust with icing sugar.

Serves 8.

MIDDLE EASTERN SLICES

375 g (12 oz) cottage cheese
155 ml (5 fl oz/$\frac{2}{3}$ cup) buttermilk
4 eggs
60 g (2 oz/$\frac{1}{4}$ cup) butter, melted
6 teaspoons clear honey
6 teaspoons caster sugar
185 g (6 oz/$\frac{1}{2}$ cup) self-raising flour
SYRUP:
155 g (5 oz/$\frac{2}{3}$ cup) granulated sugar
1 teaspoon rose water or orange flower water
TO SERVE:
orange segments and strips of peel
470 ml (15 fl oz/1$\frac{3}{4}$ cups) Greek style yogurt

Preheat oven to 190C (375F/Gas 5). Lightly grease a 20 cm (8 in) square cake tin and line with non-stick baking parchment.

In a large bowl, beat cottage cheese. Gradually add buttermilk until evenly blended. Beat in eggs and melted butter. Stir in honey, caster sugar and flour. Beat until smooth. Turn into cake tin and bake in the oven for 35 minutes.

To make syrup, put granulated sugar and rose water or orange flower water into a saucepan with 155 ml (5 fl oz/$\frac{2}{3}$ cup) water. Bring to boil and simmer until sugar has dissolved. Pour syrup over the warm cheesecake and leave to soak in while the cheesecake cools. When cool, cut cheesecake into fingers, decorate with orange segments and peel, and serve with yogurt.

Serves 8–10.

PASKHA

750 g (1½ lb) Ricotta cheese	
155 ml (5 fl oz/⅔ cup) thick sour cream	
90 g (3 oz/⅓ cup) soft unsalted butter	
60 g (2 oz/¼ cup) caster sugar	
6 teaspoons clear honey	
3 teaspoons rose water	
60 g (2 oz/½ cup) ground almonds	
90 g (3 oz/½ cup) seedless raisins	
90 g (3 oz/½ cup) mixed citrus peel	
60 g (2 oz/⅓ cup) chopped glacé cherries	
TO DECORATE:	
mixed glacé fruits	

Line a new clay flower pot, capacity 1 litre (32 fl oz/4 cups), with a double layer of cheesecloth or muslin, leaving the cloth overlapping the edges of the pot by 5 cm (2 in) all the way round.

In a bowl, beat cheese, sour cream and butter until smooth. Add sugar, honey, rose water and ground almonds and beat until smooth. Stir in raisins, mixed citrus peel and chopped glacé cherries. Spoon into lined flower pot and fold edges of cheesecloth or muslin into centre.

Stand flower pot on a saucer, place a smaller saucer on top, weight down and leave in the refrigerator for 24 hours.

To decorate, turn out onto a round serving dish and decorate with mixed glacé fruits.

Serves 8–10.

— POLISH CHEESECAKE —

1 quantity Sweet Shortcrust Pastry, see page 13
FILLING:
750 g (1½ lb) Ricotta cheese
155 ml (5 fl oz/⅔ cup) whipping cream
90 g (3 oz/⅓ cup) caster sugar
3 teaspoons plain flour
3 eggs
30 g (1 oz/2 tablespoons) sultanas
3 teaspoons orange flower water

Preheat oven to 200C (400F/Gas 6). Lightly grease a 22.5 cm (9 in) round, loose-bottomed cake tin. Roll out pastry on a lightly floured surface to a thickness of 0.3 cm (⅛ in) and use to line base and sides of tin. Prick with a fork and refrigerate while preparing filling. Reserve trimmings.

To make filling, beat cheese, cream, sugar, flour and eggs in a bowl. Add sultanas and orange flower water. Blend until smooth, then turn into cake tin.

Roll out pastry trimmings and cut into strips. Arrange strips in a lattice design over filling.

Bake in the oven for 20 minutes, then lower oven temperature to 180C (350F/Gas 4) and bake for a further 45 minutes. Allow to cool before removing from cake tin.

Serves 10–12.

PRUNE CHEESECAKE

90 g (3 oz/⅓ cup) butter
185 g (6 oz/1⅔ cups) semi-sweet biscuit crumbs
30 g (1 oz/¼ cup) ground walnuts
FILLING:
185 g (6 oz) small prunes
125 ml (4 fl oz/½ cup) Armagnac or French brandy
500 g (1 lb) medium fat curd cheese
315 ml (10 fl oz/1¼ cups) thick sour cream
2 eggs
90 g (3 oz/⅓ cup) caster sugar
6 teaspoons plain flour
TO DECORATE:
60 g (2 oz/⅓ cup) icing sugar

Put prunes for filling in a bowl, cover with boiling water and leave to soak for 15 minutes. Pour water away, transfer prunes to a jar, cover with Armagnac or brandy and leave for 24 hours.

Next day, preheat oven to 180C (350F/Gas 4). Grease and line a 20 cm (8 in) round, spring-form cake tin. In a saucepan, melt butter, then stir in biscuit crumbs and ground walnuts. Mix well, then press into base of cake tin.

In a bowl, blend together cheese, sour cream and eggs. Add caster sugar and flour and beat until smooth.

Reserve 5 of the prunes for decoration. Remove stones from remainder, then chop prunes and add to cheese mixture. Pour in half the prune juice (use remainder in a fruit salad). Turn into cake tin and bake in oven for 45 minutes. Leave to cool.

To decorate, dust surface of cheesecake with icing sugar. Cut reserved prunes in half lengthwise, remove stones, then arrange prunes, cut side down, in a flower pattern on cheesecake.

Serves 8–10.

RUSSIAN VATRUSHKI

1 quantity Sweet Shortcrust Pastry, see page 13

FILLING:

500 g (1 lb) medium fat curd cheese

90 g (3 oz/½ cup) icing sugar, plus extra for dusting

90 g (3 oz/⅓ cup) soft butter

90 ml (3 fl oz/⅓ cup) whipping cream

3 teaspoons plain flour

1 egg

60 g (2 oz/½ cup) toasted flaked almonds

60 g (2 oz/½ cup) chopped walnuts

60 g (2 oz/½ cup) chopped mixed glacé fruits

60 g (2 oz/⅓ cup) raisins

Preheat oven to 180C (350F/Gas 4). Grease a 22.5 cm (9 in) round, loose-bottomed cake tin. Roll out pastry on a lightly floured surface to a thickness of 0.5 cm (¼ in) and use to line base and sides of tin. Prick with a fork and refrigerate.

To make filling, beat cheese, icing sugar, butter and cream in a bowl. Beat in flour and egg until smooth. Stir in flaked almonds, walnuts, glacé fruits and raisins.

Turn into cake tin and bake in the oven for 50 minutes. Leave to stand until cool. Dust with icing sugar. This cheesecake is traditionally served with black coffee.

Serves 10–12.

CITRUS CHEESECAKE

60 g (2 oz/¼ cup) butter	
125 g (4 oz/1¼ cups) digestive biscuit crumbs	

FILLING:

3 oranges

2 lemons

220 g (7 oz) low fat soft cheese

155 ml (5 fl oz/⅔ cup) natural yogurt

155 ml (5 fl oz/⅔ cup) whipping cream

4 teaspoons powdered gelatine

2 eggs

6 teaspoons clear honey

TOPPING:

8 teaspoons caster sugar

3 teaspoons cornflour

1 kiwi fruit, sliced

125 g (4 oz) black grapes

Grease and line a 20 cm (8 in) round, loose-bottomed cake tin. In a saucepan, melt butter, then stir in crumbs. Mix, then press into tin.

Finely grate peel from 2 oranges and 2 lemons. In a bowl, mix together cheese, yogurt and peel. Whip cream and fold into cheese.

Sprinkle gelatine over 2 tablespoons water in a small bowl and leave to soften for 2–3 minutes. Stand the bowl in a pan of hot water and stir until dissolved and hot. Using a rotary or hand-held whisk, beat eggs and honey in a bowl until thick enough to hold trail of whisk.

Stir gelatine into cheese mixture, then fold in eggs. Turn into tin and leave to set in refrigerator.

Meanwhile, divide oranges into segments, reserving any juice in a pan. Squeeze in juice from lemons. Add sugar and bring to boil. Mix cornflour with 4 tablespoons water, then stir into juice and simmer until thickened. Cool slightly.

Spread on cake; cool. Decorate with orange, kiwi fruit and grapes.

Serves 8.

—— COTTAGE CHEESECAKE ——

125 g (4 oz/½ cup) butter

6 teaspoons light soft brown sugar

250 g (8 oz/1⅔ cups) rolled oats

FILLING:

500 g (1 lb) cottage cheese

155 ml (5 fl oz/⅔ cup) thick sour cream

2 ripe bananas, sliced

90 g (3 oz/⅓ cup) light soft brown sugar

2 eggs

6 teaspoons plain flour

few drops vanilla essence

Preheat oven to 180C (350F/Gas 4). Grease and line a 20 cm (8 in) round, loose-bottomed cake tin. In a saucepan, melt butter, then stir in sugar and rolled oats. Mix well, then spread half the mixture into cake tin.

In a bowl, beat cheese, sour cream, bananas, sugar, eggs, flour and vanilla essence until smooth. Spoon into cake tin.

Sprinkle remaining oat mixture over top, then bake in the oven for 50 minutes. Leave to cool before removing from tin.

Serves 8–10.

APPLE CHEESECAKE

1 quantity Cheesecake Pastry, see page 12

FILLING:

500 g (1 lb) cottage cheese

155 ml (5 fl oz/$\frac{2}{3}$ cup) thick sour cream

90 g (3 oz/$\frac{1}{3}$ cup) caster sugar

2 eggs

3 teaspoons plain flour

pinch of mixed spice

finely grated peel and juice of 1 lemon

500 g (1 lb) cooking apples

TOPPING:

90 g (3 oz/$2\frac{1}{2}$ cups) bran flakes

1 tablespoon icing sugar, plus extra for dusting

Preheat oven to 190C (375F/Gas 5). Grease a 22.5 cm (9 in) pie dish. Roll out pastry on a lightly floured surface to a thickness of 0.5 cm ($\frac{1}{4}$ in) and use to line the pie dish. Prick with a fork, then refrigerate while preparing filling.

In a bowl, beat cheese, sour cream, sugar, eggs, flour and mixed spice. Stir in lemon peel and juice.

Peel, core and chop apples. Spread half in pie dish, pour over cheese mixture, then cover with remaining chopped apple.

Put bran flakes and icing sugar into a plastic bag and shake. Spread over surface of cheesecake. Bake in the oven for 45 minutes. Leave to cool before cutting. Dust with icing sugar to serve.

Serves 8–10.

—— BUTTERMILK CHEESECAKE ——

90 g (3 oz/⅓ cup) butter

185 g (6 oz/1⅔ cups) semi-sweet biscuit crumbs

FILLING:

500 g (1 lb) Ricotta cheese

125 ml (4 fl oz/½ cup) buttermilk

2 eggs

90 g (3 oz/⅓ cup) caster sugar

few drops vanilla essence

3 teaspoons plain flour

TO DECORATE:

470 ml (15 fl oz/1¾ cups) Greek style yogurt

lemon twists

Preheat oven to 160C (325F/Gas 3). Grease a 20 cm (8 in) round, spring-form cake tin. In a saucepan, melt butter, then stir in biscuit crumbs. Mix well, then press into base of cake tin.

In a bowl, blend cheese with a quarter of buttermilk until smooth. Gradually add remaining buttermilk until evenly blended. Beat in eggs, one at a time, then sugar, vanilla essence and flour. Turn into cake tin and bake in oven for 50 minutes. Leave to cool in tin.

To decorate, spread yogurt over top of cheesecake, making peaks with the back of a spoon. Arrange twists of lemon around the edge of the cheesecake.

Serves 8–10.

— TOFU BANANA CHEESECAKE —

60 g (2 oz/¼ cup) butter

125 g (4 oz/1¼ cups) rich tea biscuit crumbs

FILLING:

375 g (12 oz) tofu, cut into small pieces

375 g (12 oz) cottage cheese

2 ripe bananas, chopped

3 teaspoons clear honey

3 teaspoons plain flour

finely grated peel and juice of 1 lime

TO DECORATE:

2 bananas

60 g (2 oz/¼ cup) apricot jam

3 teaspoons lemon juice

30 g (1 oz) angelica

Preheat oven to 180C (350F/Gas 4). Grease and line a 20 cm (8 in) round, loose-bottomed cake tin. In a saucepan, melt butter, then add biscuit crumbs. Mix well, then press into base of cake tin.

Put tofu into a bowl and stir in cheese, chopped bananas, honey and flour. Beat well, then stir in lime peel and juice. Spoon onto biscuit base and bake in the oven for 45 minutes.

To decorate, slice bananas diagonally into oval shapes. Arrange slices around edge of cheesecake. Put jam into a saucepan with lemon juice. Bring to the boil, then brush over the banana slices. Cut angelica into leaf shapes and arrange on banana slices.

Serves 8–10.

— BLACKBERRY CHEESECAKE —

125 g (4 oz/½ cup) butter

6 teaspoons light soft brown sugar

250 g (8 oz/2 cups) rolled oats

FILLING:

500 g (1 lb) Ricotta cheese

155 ml (5 fl oz/⅔ cup) thick sour cream

90 g (3 oz/⅓ cup) caster sugar

2 eggs

3 teaspoons plain flour

pinch of ground cloves

500 g (1 lb) cooking apples

90 g (3 oz) blackberries, thawed
if frozen

TOPPING:

375 g (12 oz) blackberries, thawed
if frozen

90 g (3 oz/¼ cup) redcurrant jelly

155 ml (5 fl oz/⅔ cup) whipping cream

10 sprigs of mint

Preheat oven to 180C (350F/Gas 4). Grease and line a 20 cm (8 in) round, loose-bottomed cake tin. In a saucepan, melt butter, then stir in brown sugar and oats. Mix well, then press into cake tin.

In a bowl, beat cheese, sour cream, sugar and eggs. Add flour and cloves and beat until smooth. Peel, core and chop apples. Stir into cheese with the 90 g (3 oz) blackberries. Spoon onto biscuit base and bake in the oven for 45 minutes. Leave to cool before removing from tin.

To make topping, arrange blackberries in centre of cheesecake. Melt redcurrant jelly in a small saucepan, then brush over blackberries. Whip cream and pipe a border of 10 rosettes around edge of cheesecake. Top each rosette with a mint sprig.

Serves 8–10.

PLUM CHEESECAKE

1 quantity Cheesecake Pastry, see page 12

FILLING:

220 g (7 oz) Ricotta cheese

1 egg

60 g (2 oz/¼ cup) caster sugar

155 ml (5 fl oz/⅔ cup) natural yogurt

3 teaspoons lemon juice

½ teaspoon ground cinnamon

500 g (1 lb) dark plums, halved

TOPPING:

60 g (2 oz/½ cup) plain flour

30 g (1 oz/2 tablespoons) light Muscovado sugar

30 g (1 oz/6 teaspoons) cool butter

Preheat oven to 180C (350F/Gas 4). Grease a 20 cm (8 in) pie dish. Roll out pastry on a lightly floured surface to a thickness of 0.5 cm (¼ in) and use to line pie dish. Prick with a fork, then refrigerate while preparing filling.

In a bowl, beat cheese, egg, sugar and yogurt. Add lemon juice and cinnamon and beat until smooth.

Arrange half the plums in pastry case and spread cheese mixture over the top. Cover with remaining plums.

To make topping, put flour and sugar into a bowl and rub in butter until mixture resembles breadcrumbs. Sprinkle topping over plums and bake in the oven for 50 minutes. Leave to cool before cutting.

Serves 6–8.

DUBLIN CURD CAKE

1 quantity Cheesecake Pastry, see page 12

FILLING:

375 g (12 oz) medium fat curd cheese or strained cottage cheese

155 ml (5 fl oz/⅔ cup) thick sour cream

60 g (2 oz/¼ cup) caster sugar

2 eggs

3 teaspoons plain flour

60 g (2 oz/¼ cup) butter, melted

TOPPING:

60 g (2 oz/⅓ cup) raisins

TO SERVE:

damson jam

Preheat oven to 190C (375F/Gas 5). Grease a 22.5 cm (9 in) pie dish.

Roll out pastry on a lightly floured surface to a thickness of 0.5 cm (¼ in) and use to line pie dish. Prick with a fork and refrigerate while preparing filling.

In a bowl, beat curd or cottage cheese, sour cream, sugar and eggs. Add flour and melted butter and beat until smooth.

Pour into pie dish, sprinkle raisins over top, then bake in the oven for 40 minutes.

Serve warm or cold, with a little damson jam spooned onto each portion.

Serves 8.

GINGER CURD CAKE

60 g (2 oz/¼ cup) butter

185 g (6 oz/1⅔ cups) ginger biscuit crumbs

FILLING:

750 g (1½ lb) medium fat curd cheese

2 eggs

9 teaspoons clear honey

6 teaspoons stem ginger syrup

finely grated peel and juice of 1 orange

TO DECORATE:

8-10 pieces stem ginger

60 g (2 oz) angelica, cut into even-sized pieces

Preheat oven to 160C (325F/Gas 3). Grease and line a 22.5 cm (9 in) round, loose-bottomed cake tin. In a saucepan, melt butter, then stir in biscuit crumbs. Mix well, then press into base of cake tin.

In a bowl, beat cheese, eggs, honey, ginger syrup and orange peel. Stir in orange juice and beat until smooth. Spoon onto biscuit base and bake in the oven for 1¼ hours. Leave to cool before removing from tin.

To decorate, slice each piece of stem ginger into 5. Arrange ginger slices in groups of 5, one group for each portion. Place 2 or 3 pieces of angelica on each group of ginger slices.

Serves 8-10.

— RHUBARB & CUSTARD CAKE —

60 g (2 oz/¼ cup) butter
125 g (4 oz/1¼ cups) ginger biscuit crumbs
FILLING:
6 teaspoons cornflour
250 ml (8 fl oz/1 cup) milk
3 egg yolks
few drops vanilla essence
4 teaspoons powdered gelatine
375 g (12 oz) medium fat soft cheese
TOPPING:
1 kg (2 lb) rhubarb
90 g (3 oz/⅓ cup) caster sugar
625 ml (20 fl oz/2½ cups) boiling water

Grease a 22.5 cm (9 in) round, loose-bottomed cake tin. In a saucepan, melt butter, then stir in biscuit crumbs. Mix well, then press into base of cake tin.

In a heatproof bowl, mix cornflour with 3 tablespoons milk. Add egg yolks and vanilla essence. Stir well. In a saucepan, bring remaining milk to the boil. Pour into bowl and stir well, then pour back into saucepan and simmer to thicken.

Sprinkle gelatine over 2 tablespoons water in a small bowl and leave to soften for 2–3 minutes. Stir into custard and leave to cool.

Put cheese in a bowl. When custard has cooled and nearly set, blend a little at a time into cheese. Pour onto biscuit base and leave to set in the refrigerator for 2–3 hours.

Meanwhile, prepare topping. Cut rhubarb into 6 cm (2½ in) slices. Arrange in a heatproof dish, sprinkle over sugar and pour over boiling water. Cover and leave to cook in its own heat for 25–30 minutes.

When cheesecake has set, remove from tin. Remove rhubarb from liquid and drain on a wire rack. Arrange pieces in a fan shape around edge of cheesecake. Chill.

Serves 8.

CAROUSEL DE FROMAGE

500 g (1 lb) medium fat soft cheese
315 ml (10 fl oz/1 ¼ cups) whipping cream
90 g (3 oz/⅓ cup) caster sugar
3 eggs
few drops vanilla essence
TO DECORATE:
2 eating apples
2 pears
185 g (6 oz) strawberries
185 g (6 oz) raspberries
125 g (4 oz) black grapes
2 oranges
1 kiwi fruit
155 ml (5 fl oz/⅔ cup) whipping cream
10 sprigs of mint

Preheat oven to 190C (375F/Gas 5). Grease a 22.5 cm (9 in) ring mould. In a bowl, beat cheese and cream until smooth. Add sugar, eggs and vanilla essence and blend evenly. Spoon into ring mould.

Stand ring mould in a roasting tin and add enough boiling water to come halfway up sides of ring mould. Cover with aluminium foil and bake in the oven for 50 minutes. To test ring, pierce with a skewer – if it comes away cleanly the ring is cooked. Leave to cool before turning out.

To decorate, cut the fruits into even-sized pieces. Arrange them in centre of ring. Whip cream and pipe 10 rosettes of cream around edge. Top each with a sprig of mint.

Serves 8–10.

OLD-FASHIONED CHEESECAKE

125 g (4 oz/½ cup) butter

60 g (2 oz/¼ cup) light soft brown sugar

125 g (4 oz/1 cup) wholewheat flour

125 g (4 oz/1 cup) rolled oats

FILLING:

375 g (12 oz) medium fat soft cheese

315 ml (10 fl oz/1¼ cups) buttermilk

2 eggs

60 g (2 oz/¼ cup) light soft brown sugar

3 teaspoons plain flour

1 teaspoon bicarbonate of soda

TOPPING:

90 g (3 oz) macaroons, broken into pieces

Preheat oven to 190C (375F/Gas 5). Grease a 20 cm (8 in) pie dish. In saucepan, melt butter, then stir in sugar, flour and oats. Mix well, then press mixture into base and up sides of pie dish.

To make filling, beat cheese and buttermilk in a bowl. Add eggs and sugar and beat until smooth. Sift flour and bicarbonate of soda over mixture and stir in well.

Spoon into pie dish and sprinkle broken macaroons over top. Bake in the oven for 35 minutes. Leave the cheesecake to cool completely before cutting.

Serves 6–8.

——— MOSS TOP CHEESECAKE ———

125 g (4 oz/½ cup) butter

250 g (8 oz/2¼ cups) semi-sweet biscuit crumbs

FILLING:

500 g (1 lb) medium fat soft cheese

155 ml (5 fl oz/⅔ cup) whipping cream

90 g (3 oz/⅓ cup) caster sugar

2 eggs

60 g (2 oz/½ cup) chopped dried apricots

MOSS TOPPING:

185 g (6 oz/¾ cup) soft butter

125 g (4 oz/½ cup) caster sugar

1 egg, beaten

few drops vanilla essence

345 g (11 oz/2¾ cups) plain flour

TO DECORATE:

30 g (1 oz/2 tablespoons) icing sugar

Preheat oven to 180C (350F/Gas 4). Grease and line a 20 cm (8 in) round, spring-form cake tin. In a saucepan, melt butter, then stir in biscuit crumbs. Mix well, then press into base and up sides of cake tin.

To make filling, beat cheese and cream in a bowl. Add sugar and eggs and beat for 2–3 minutes. Stir in chopped apricots, then spoon into cake tin. Bake in the oven for 30 minutes.

Meanwhile, prepare topping. In a bowl, beat butter and sugar until pale in colour. Gradually beat in beaten egg, then stir in vanilla essence and flour. Put mixture into a biscuit press fitted with a worm cast disc.

Force the moss topping through the press onto the partially cooked cheesecake. Return it to the oven and bake for a further 20 minutes until both cheesecake and topping are cooked. Leave to cool before releasing the tin. Dust with icing sugar before serving.

Serves 8–10.

——— MARBLED CHEESECAKE ———

60 g (2 oz/¼ cup) butter

185 g (6 oz/1⅔ cups) digestive biscuit crumbs

FILLING:

750 g (1½ lb) medium fat soft cheese

90 g (3 oz/⅓ cup) caster sugar

3 teaspoons plain flour

3 eggs

few drops vanilla essence

90 g (3 oz) plain (dark) chocolate, broken into pieces

Preheat oven to 180C (350F/Gas 4). Grease a 20 cm (8 in) round, loose-bottomed cake tin. In a saucepan, melt butter, then stir in biscuit crumbs. Mix well, then press the mixture into base of cake tin.

In a bowl, beat cheese, sugar, flour, eggs and vanilla essence. Spoon onto biscuit base and set aside.

Melt chocolate in the top of a double boiler or a bowl set over a saucepan of simmering water. Pour melted chocolate in a thin stream over cheese mixture. Using the handle of a teaspoon, swirl the 2 mixtures to create a marbled effect.

Bake in the oven for 45 minutes. Leave cheesecake to cool before removing from the tin.

Serves 8–10.

EASTER CHEESECAKE

1 quantity Sweet Shortcrust Pastry, see page 13

FILLING:

500 g (1 lb) medium fat curd cheese

155 ml (5 fl oz/⅔ cup) whipping cream

2 eggs

90 g (3 oz/⅓ cup) butter

90 g (3 oz/⅓ cup) caster sugar

finely grated peel and juice of 1 lemon

pinch of ground mace

60 g (2 oz/⅓ cup) currants

TO GLAZE:

1 egg yolk

generous pinch of salt

TO SERVE:

pouring cream

Grease a 22.5 cm (9 in) loose-bottomed flan tin. Roll out pastry on a lightly floured surface and use to line the flan tin. Prick with a fork and refrigerate while preparing filling. Reserve pastry trimmings.

Meanwhile, heat oven to 190C (375F/Gas 5). In a bowl, beat cheese and cream until smooth. Add eggs, butter and sugar. Beat well, then add lemon peel and juice and ground mace. Stir in currants, then turn into pastry case.

Roll out pastry trimmings and cut into 1 cm (½ in) strips. Arrange strips in a lattice pattern over filling. Mix together egg yolk and salt and brush over pastry strips. Bake in the oven for 40 minutes. Serve warm, with pouring cream.

Serves 6–8.

—— CURD CHEESE POPETTES ——

90 g (3 oz/⅓ cup) butter
155 g (5 oz/5¼ cups) crushed cornflakes
FILLING:
375 g (12 oz) medium fat curd cheese
155 ml (5 fl oz/⅔ cup) thick sour cream
3 eggs, separated
90 g (3 oz/⅓ cup) caster sugar
TO DECORATE:
250 g (8 oz) small strawberries

In a small saucepan, melt butter, then stir in crushed cornflakes. Mix well, then press mixture into 18 individual tartlet tins, dividing it equally between them.

In a bowl, beat cheese and sour cream until smooth. Add egg yolks and 60 g (2 oz/¼ cup) sugar and mix well.

Whisk egg whites in a separate bowl with remaining sugar until firm. Fold into cheese mixture with a large metal spoon.

Divide cheese mixture between moulds and decorate each with a strawberry.

Makes 18.

Note: Serve these tartlets at children's parties or as a tea time treat.

- BLACKCURRANT INDIVIDUALS -

6 tablespoons blackcurrant preserve
250 g (8 oz) medium fat curd cheese
90 ml (3 fl oz/⅓ cup) thick sour cream
finely grated peel and juice of ½ a lemon
1 egg
9 teaspoons caster sugar
TO DECORATE:
6 sprigs of mint
TO SERVE:
155 ml (5 fl oz/⅔ cup) whipping cream

Preheat oven to 180C (350F/Gas 4). Spread 1 tablespoon blackcurrant preserve into bottom of 6 ramekin dishes. Place ramekins in a roasting tin and set aside.

In a bowl, beat cheese and sour cream. Add lemon peel and juice, egg and sugar, and beat until smooth. Spoon mixture into ramekin dishes, dividing it equally between them.

Pour enough boiling water into roasting tin to come halfway up sides of ramekin dishes. Bake in the oven for 35 minutes. Leave to cool completely.

To serve, run the blade of a small knife around edge of each ramekin dish and turn out onto a serving dish. Decorate each cheesecake with a spring of mint and serve with loosely whipped cream.

Serves 6.

MANGO CHEESECAKE

60 g (2 oz/¼ cup) butter

155 g (5 oz/1⅓ cups) digestive biscuit crumbs

FILLING:

250 g (8 oz) full fat soft cheese

155 ml (5 fl oz/⅔ cup) natural yogurt

155 ml (5 fl oz/⅔ cup) thick sour cream

2 eggs, separated

90 g (3 oz/⅓ cup) caster sugar

3 teaspoons powdered gelatine

250 g (8 oz) raspberries

TO DECORATE:

440 g (14 oz) can mango in syrup

250 g (8 oz) raspberries

155 ml (5 fl oz/⅔ cup) whipping cream

8-10 sprigs of mint

Grease and line a 22.5 cm (9 in) round, loose-bottomed cake tin. In a saucepan, melt butter, then stir in biscuit crumbs. Mix well, then press into cake tin.

To make filling, beat cheese and yogurt in a bowl. Add sour cream, egg yolks and 60 g (2 oz/¼ cup) sugar and beat until smooth.

Sprinkle gelatine over 2 tablespoons water in a small bowl and leave to soften for 2–3 minutes. Stand the bowl in a saucepan of hot water and stir until dissolved and quite hot. Stir into cheese mixture.

Whisk egg whites in a bowl with remaining sugar until firm. Fold into cheese mixture with the raspberries. Turn into cake tin and leave to set in the refrigerator for 2–3 hours.

To decorate, slice mango into thin strips and arrange in a fan shape on the top of the cheesecake. Arrange raspberries in centre. Whip cream and pipe 8–10 rosettes around the edge. Top each with a sprig of mint.

Serves 8 10.

PUMPKIN CHEESECAKE

1 quantity Cheesecake Pastry, see
page 12

FILLING:

1 kg (2 lb) fresh pumpkin or 500 g (1 lb)
canned pumpkin purée

large pinch of salt

500 g (1 lb) full fat soft cheese

155 g (5 oz/⅔ cup) caster sugar

2 eggs

1½ teaspoons ground cinnamon

1 teaspoon ground allspice

¼ teaspoon ground ginger

¼ teaspoon ground mace

Grease a 20 cm (8 in) round, loose-bottomed cake tin. Roll out pastry on a lightly floured surface to a thickness of 0.5 cm (¼ in) and use to line the base of cake tin. Prick with a fork, then refrigerate while preparing filling.

If using fresh pumpkin, cut away outer skin. Collect seeds in a clean tea towel and set aside. Chop flesh into even-sized pieces. Put flesh into a large saucepan, add salt and 90 ml (3 fl oz/⅓ cup) water. Cover, bring to the boil and simmer for 25 minutes, stirring occasionally. Drain and leave to cool in a colander.

Meanwhile, preheat oven to 180C (350F/Gas 4). In a bowl, beat cheese, sugar and eggs until smooth.

Weigh cooked pumpkin – you need 500 g (1 lb). Add pumpkin or pumpkin purée to cheese mixture with spices. Beat until smooth. Turn into cake tin and bake in the oven for 45 minutes. Leave to cool before removing from tin.

Meanwhile, rub the pumpkin seeds in the tea towel until any flesh has been rubbed off. Spread seeds out on a baking sheet and grill under a high heat for 10–12 minutes. Arrange on the cheesecake.

Serves 8–10.

—— ICE-BOX CHEESECAKE ——

90 g (3 oz/⅓ cup) butter
185 g (6 oz/1⅔ cups) plain biscuit crumbs
½ teaspoon ground ginger
FILLING:
500 g (1 lb) full fat soft cheese
grated peel and juice of 1 lemon
4 eggs, separated
125 g (4 oz/½ cup) caster sugar
4 teaspoons powdered gelatine
315 ml (10 fl oz/1¼ cups) whipping cream
TO DECORATE:
440 g (14 oz) can pineapple rings
220 g (7 oz) red cherries
angelica 'leaves'

Grease and line a 20 cm (8 in) round, loose-bottomed cake tin. In a saucepan, melt butter, then stir in crumbs and ginger. Mix well, then press into base of cake tin.

In a bowl, beat cheese, lemon peel and juice, egg yolks and 60 g (2 oz/¼ cup) caster sugar until smooth.

Sprinkle gelatine over 2 tablespoons water in a small bowl and leave to soften for 2–3 minutes. Stand the bowl in a saucepan of hot water and stir until dissolved and quite hot. Stir into cheese mixture.

Loosely whip cream in a bowl and fold into cheese mixture with a large metal spoon. In a separate bowl, whisk egg whites with remaining sugar until firm, then fold into mixture. Pour onto biscuit base and freeze in ice compartment for 4 hours.

To decorate, cut pineapple rings in half and arrange them around the edge of the cheesecake. Place a cherry and 2 angelica 'leaves' in the centre of every other ring.

Serves 8–10.

Note: This cheesecake can be served straight from the refrigerator.

——— LINDY'S CHEESECAKE ———

250 g (8 oz/2 cups) plain flour
60 g (2 oz/¼ cup) caster sugar
finely grated peel of ½ a lemon
155 g (5 oz/⅔ cup) cool butter, cut into walnut-sized pieces
1 egg, beaten
FILLING:
750 g (1½ lb) full fat soft cheese
250 ml (8 fl oz/1 cup) thick sour cream
155 g (5 oz/⅔ cup) caster sugar
6 teaspoons plain flour
3 eggs, plus 2 egg yolks
finely grated peel and juice of 1 orange
finely grated peel and juice of 1 lemon
few drops vanilla essence
TO SERVE:
icing sugar
strawberries

Sift flour into a large bowl and add sugar and lemon peel. Rub in butter until mixture resembles breadcrumbs. Add the egg and bring together, without overworking, to form an even dough. Put in a plastic bag and leave to rest in the refrigerator for 30 minutes.

Meanwhile, preheat oven to 240C (475F/Gas 9). Grease and line a 20 cm (8 in) round, loose-bottomed cake tin. Roll out pastry on a lightly floured surface to a thickness of 0.5 cm (¼ in) and use to line cake tin.

To make filling, beat cheese, sour cream, sugar, flour, eggs and egg yolks in a bowl. Stir in orange and lemon peel and juice, followed by vanilla essence. Beat until smooth.

Spoon mixture into pastry case and bake in the oven for 15 minutes. Lower oven temperature to 140C (275F/Gas 1) and bake for a further 50 minutes. Leave to cool before removing from tin. Dust with icing sugar and decorate with strawberries before serving.

Serves 10–12.

——— COFFEE CHEESECAKE ———

1 quantity Cheesecake Pastry, see
page 12

FILLING:

60 g (2 oz/⅓ cup) sultanas

60 ml (2 fl oz/¼ cup) Tia Maria coffee
liqueur

375 g (12 oz) full fat soft cheese

155 ml (5 fl oz/⅔ cup) whipping cream

3 eggs

30 g (1 oz/¼ cup) plain flour

6 teaspoons instant coffee granules

6 teaspoons boiling water

TOPPING:

3 teaspoons caster sugar

90 g (3 oz) plain (dark) chocolate, broken
into pieces

90 g (3 oz) full fat soft cheese

chocolate coffee beans

Roll out pastry on a lightly floured
surface to a thickness of 0.5 cm (¼
in). Place base of a 22.5 cm (9 in)
round, loose-bottomed cake tin over
pastry and cut out a circle the same
size. Grease cake tin and place
pastry in base. Prick with a fork;
refrigerate while making filling.

Put sultanas and Tia Maria into a
small saucepan, bring to boil, then
leave to cool and plump up. Meanwhile, preheat oven to 190C (375F/
Gas 5). In a bowl, beat cheese,
cream, eggs and flour until smooth.
Dissolve coffee granules in boiling
water and stir into cheese mixture.
Add sultanas. Turn into tin and
bake in the oven for 50 minutes.
Leave to cool in tin.

To make topping, put sugar into a
small saucepan with 60 ml (2 fl oz/¼
cup) water and bring to the boil.
Remove from heat and stir in
chocolate. Leave to cool. Put cheese
in a bowl, then beat in chocolate
until smooth. Spread over cheesecake and decorate with beans.

Serves 10–12.

—— RASPBERRY CHEESE ROLL ——

4 eggs
125 g (4 oz/½ cup) caster sugar
60 g (2 oz/½ cup) ground almonds
6 teaspoons plain flour
FILLING:
185 g (6 oz) full fat soft cheese
155 ml (5 fl oz/⅔ cup) whipping cream
3 teaspoons icing sugar
500 g (1 lb) raspberries
TO DECORATE:
155 ml (5 fl oz/⅔ cup) whipping cream
6-8 sprigs of mint

Preheat oven to 200C (400F/Gas 6). Grease and line a 32.5 x 22.5 cm (13 x 9 in) baking sheet. Using a rotary or hand-held whisk, beat eggs and sugar in a bowl until mixture is thick enough to hold trail of the whisk when beaters are lifted.

Sift ground almonds and flour over egg mixture and fold in with a large metal spoon. Spread out sponge mixture on the baking sheet and bake in the oven for 10–12 minutes or until springy to the touch. Turn out onto a wire rack and leave to cool.

Put cheese into a blender or food processor with cream and icing sugar and blend until smooth – do not overblend or cream will separate.

Peel greaseproof paper off sponge and spread cheese mixture over sponge. Scatter three-quarters of the raspberries over top, then roll up lightly.

To decorate, whip cream and pipe a row of rosettes along top of the cheese roll. Decorate with remaining raspberries and sprigs of mint.

Serves 6–8.

——— BOSTON CHEESECAKE ———

90 g (3 oz/⅓ cup) butter

250 g (8 oz/2¼ cups) rich tea biscuit crumbs

¼ teaspoon ground cinnamon

¼ teaspoon ground allspice

FILLING:

500 g (1 lb) full fat soft cheese

250 ml (8 fl oz/1 cup) thick sour cream

155 g (5 oz/⅔ cup) caster sugar

4 eggs, separated

6 teaspoons plain flour

few drops vanilla essence

finely grated peel and juice of 1 lemon

TO SERVE:

icing sugar

Preheat oven to 180C (350F/Gas 4). Grease and line a 22.5 cm (9 in) round, loose-bottomed tin. In a saucepan, melt butter, then stir in biscuit crumbs and spices. Mix well, then press into base of cake tin.

In a bowl, beat cheese, sour cream, 90 g (3 oz/⅓ cup) sugar, egg yolks, flour, vanilla essence and lemon peel and juice until smooth.

Whisk egg whites in a separate bowl with remaining sugar until stiff. Fold into cheese mixture with a large metal spoon. Turn into cake tin and bake in the oven for 1 hour.

Leave to cool before removing from the tin. To decorate, cut out 5 strips of greaseproof paper 2 cm (¾ in) wide and lay them at intervals over surface of cheesecake. Sift icing sugar over the top. Carefully remove strips and serve.

Serves 10–12.

— STRAWBERRY SMOOTH CAKE —

1 quantity Cheesecake Pastry, see page 12

2 tablespoons strawberry jam

FILLING:

500 g (1 lb) full fat soft cheese

250 ml (8 fl oz/1 cup) thick sour cream

3 eggs, separated, plus 1 egg yolk

90 g (3 oz/⅓ cup) caster sugar

6 teaspoons plain flour

finely grated peel and juice of 1 orange

TOPPING:

375 g (12 oz) strawberries

2 tablespoons redcurrant jelly, if desired

Preheat oven to 160C (325F/Gas 3). Grease and line a 22.5 cm (9 in) round, loose-bottomed cake tin. Roll out pastry on a lightly floured surface to a thickness of 0.5 cm (¼ in) and use to line base of tin. Prick with a fork, then spread strawberry jam over pastry. Refrigerate while making filling.

In a bowl, beat cheese, sour cream, egg yolks, 60 g (2 oz/¼ cup) sugar, flour, orange peel and juice until smooth.

Whisk egg whites in a separate bowl with remaining sugar until firm. Fold into cheese mixture using a large metal spoon. Turn into tin and bake near the bottom of the oven for 1 hour. Leave to cool before removing from tin.

To decorate, reserve one strawberry, then slice rest into 0.5 cm (¼ in) slices. Arrange slices, pointed ends outwards, around edge of cheesecake. Repeat with more circles, working in towards centre, overlapping layers slightly. Place strawberry in centre. Melt redcurrant jelly in a small saucepan and use to glaze strawberries, if desired.

Serves 8–10.

— MANHATTAN CHEESECAKE

60 g (2 oz/¼ cup) butter
125 g (4 oz/1¼ cups) digestive biscuit crumbs
FILLING:
250 g (8 oz) full fat soft cheese
250 g (8 oz) cottage cheese
170 ml (5½ fl oz/⅔ cup) evaporated milk
few drops vanilla essence
pinch of salt
6 teaspoons plain flour
3 teaspoons lemon juice
125 g (4 oz/½ cup) caster sugar
3 eggs, separated
TOPPING:
icing sugar

Preheat oven to 180C (350F/Gas 4). Grease and line a 22.5 cm (9 in) round, loose-bottomed cake tin. In a saucepan, melt butter, then stir in biscuit crumbs. Mix well, then press into base of cake tin.

In a bowl, beat all filling ingredients except sugar and egg whites. Whisk egg whites and sugar in a separate bowl until firm. Fold beaten egg into cheese mixture with a metal spoon. Turn into cake tin and bake in the oven for 1 hour. Leave to cool before removing from tin, then chill. Dust with icing sugar before serving.

Serves 10–12.

Variation: Top the cheesecake with fresh fruit of your choice instead of icing sugar, if preferred.

TROPICAL CHEESECAKE

1 quantity Plain Sponge Border, see
page 10

60 g (2 oz/¼ cup) butter

155 g (5 oz/1⅓ cups) ginger biscuit crumbs

FILLING:

250 g (8 oz) full fat soft cheese

250 g (8 oz/1 cup) Greek style yogurt

2 eggs, separated

90 g (3 oz/⅓ cup) caster sugar

3 teaspoons powdered gelatine

155 ml (5 fl oz/⅔ cup) whipping cream

TOPPING:

500 g (1 lb) assorted fruit, such as mangoes,
kiwi fruit, passion fruit, blueberries,
pineapple, mandarin oranges, bananas

90 g (3 oz/¼ cup) redcurrant jelly,
if desired

Cut sponge border to same height as a 22.5 cm (9 in) round, loose-bottomed cake tin and arrange round sides of tin. Line base of tin with greaseproof paper. In a saucepan, melt butter, then stir in biscuit crumbs. Mix well, then press into base of cake tin.

In a bowl, beat cheese, yogurt, egg yolks and 30 g (1 oz/5 teaspoons) sugar until smooth.

Sprinkle gelatine over 2 table-spoons water in a small bowl and leave to soften for 2–3 minutes. Stand the bowl in a saucepan of hot water and stir until dissolved and quite hot. Stir into cheese mixture.

Whip cream in a bowl and fold into cheese mixture with a large spoon. Whisk egg whites in a separate bowl with remaining sugar until firm. Fold into cheese, turn into tin and refrigerate for 2–3 hours.

To decorate, cut fruit into even-sized pieces and arrange on cheese-cake. Melt redcurrant jelly in a saucepan and brush over fruit to glaze, if desired.

Serves 8–10.

— STRAWBERRY CHEESE FLAN —

1 quantity Cheesecake Pastry, see page 12

FILLING:

185 g (6 oz) full fat soft cheese

finely grated peel and juice of 1 orange

few drops vanilla essence

3 egg yolks

60 g (2 oz/¼ cup) caster sugar

155 ml (5 fl oz/⅔ cup) whipping cream

TOPPING:

375 g (12 oz) strawberries

90 g (3 oz/¼ cup) strawberry jam

Preheat oven to 200C (400F/Gas 6). Grease a 22.5 cm (9 in) flan dish. Roll out pastry on a lightly floured surface to a thickness of 0.5 cm (¼ in) and use to line the dish. Refrigerate for 30 minutes, then bake blind in the oven for 35 minutes.

Meanwhile, make filling. In a bowl, beat cheese, orange peel and juice and vanilla essence until smooth. In a separate bowl, beat egg yolks and sugar until smooth and pale in colour.

Put cream in a saucepan and bring to the boil, then stir into yolks (the yolks and cream will thicken in their own heat). Leave to cool slightly, then blend into cheese mixture until well mixed and light. Spread in the cooked flan case.

Arrange strawberries, pointed end upwards, over filling. Melt strawberry jam in a saucepan with 1 tablespoon water, then brush over strawberries to glaze.

Serves 6.

APRICOT CHEESECAKE

90 g (3 oz/⅓ cup) butter

185 g (6 oz/1⅔ cups) digestive biscuit crumbs

FILLING:

250 g (8 oz) low fat soft cheese

155 ml (5 fl oz/⅔ cup) natural yogurt

90 g (3 oz/¾ cup) ground almonds

125 g (4 oz/½ cup) caster sugar

155 ml (5 fl oz/⅔ cup) whipping cream

3 teaspoons powdered gelatine

2 eggs

few drops almond essence

TO DECORATE:

440 g (14 oz) can apricot halves

155 ml (5 fl oz/⅔ cup) whipping cream

Grease and line a 20 cm (8 in) square cake tin. In a saucepan, melt butter, then stir in biscuit crumbs. Mix well, then press into base of cake tin.

In a bowl, beat cheese, yogurt, ground almonds and 60 g (2 oz/¼ cup) sugar until smooth. Loosely whip cream in a separate bowl, then fold into cheese mixture.

Sprinkle gelatine over 2 tablespoons water in a small bowl and leave to soften for 2–3 minutes. Stand the bowl in a saucepan of hot water and stir until dissolved and quite hot. Stir into cheese mixture.

Using a rotary or hand-held whisk, beat eggs, almond essence and remaining sugar in a bowl until mixture is thick enough to hold trail of the whisk when beaters are lifted. Fold beaten eggs into cheese mixture and pour onto biscuit base. Leave to set in the refrigerator for 2–3 hours.

To decorate, cut cheesecake into sixteen 5 cm (2 in) squares. Drain apricot halves and place one in centre of each square. Whip the cream and pipe a border of cream around edge of each square.

Serves 16.

— BLUEBERRY CHEESECAKE —

60 g (2 oz/½ cup) butter
125 g (4 oz/1½ cups) digestive or other semi-sweet biscuit crumbs
6 teaspoons sweet sherry
FILLING:
375 g (12 oz) Ricotta cheese
155 ml (5 fl oz/⅓ cup) natural yogurt
90 g (3 oz/⅓ cup) sugar
3 teaspoons lemon juice
2 eggs, separated
500 g (1 lb) blueberries
3 teaspoons powdered gelatine
TOPPING:
90 g (3 oz/¼ cup) redcurrant jelly
TO SERVE:
sprigs of mint
155 ml (5 fl oz/⅔ cup) whipping cream

Grease a 22.5 cm (9 in) round, loose-bottomed cake tin. In a saucepan, melt butter, then stir in biscuit crumbs and sherry. Mix well, then press into base of cake tin. Leave to firm in the refrigerator.

In a bowl, beat cheese, yogurt, 60 g (2 oz/¼ cup) sugar, lemon juice and egg yolks. Gently stir in 125 g (4 oz) of the blueberries.

Sprinkle gelatine over 2 tablespoons water in a small bowl and leave to soften for 2–3 minutes. Stand the bowl in a saucepan of hot water and stir until dissolved and quite hot. Stir into cheese.

Whisk egg whites with remaining sugar until firm and smooth. Fold into cheese mixture with a large metal spoon, then spoon onto biscuit base. Leave to set in refrigerator for 2–3 hours.

To make topping, melt redcurrant jelly in a small saucepan without boiling. Stir in remaining blueberries. Mix well, spread over cheesecake and chill. Decorate with mint and serve with whipped cream.

Serves 8–10.

COEURS À LA CRÈME

1.8 litres (3 pints/7 cups) milk
155 ml (5 fl oz/⅔ cup) whipping cream
1½ teaspoons rennet
TO DECORATE:
155 ml (5 fl oz/⅔ cup) whipping cream, if desired
250 g (8 oz) strawberries

Line 6 coeur à la crème moulds with a double layer of muslin. Put milk and cream into a saucepan and warm to blood temperature (do not allow to become too hot or the milk will not curdle properly). Stir in rennet and leave for 1 hour.

When the milk has curdled, pour contents of saucepan into a jelly bag suspended over an upturned kitchen stool. Place a bowl underneath to collect the whey. Leave to drain for about 50 minutes.

Empty contents of jelly bag into a glass bowl and stir curds until smooth. Divide cheese between moulds and leave in the refrigerator until firm.

Turn out onto individual serving plates. To decorate if desired, whip cream, then pipe onto moulds. Decorate with strawberry slices.

Serves 6.

— PASSION FRUIT CHEESECAKE —

60 g (2 oz/¼ cup) butter

125 g (4 oz/1¼ cups) digestive biscuit crumbs

FILLING:

250 g (8 oz) full fat soft cheese

250 ml (8 fl oz/1 cup) Greek style yogurt

2 eggs, separated

125 g (4 oz/½ cup) caster sugar

10 passion fruit

juice of 1 lemon

4 teaspoons powdered gelatine

TOPPING:

60 ml (2 fl oz/¼ cup) orange juice

30 g (1 oz/5 teaspoons) caster sugar

6 teaspoons cornflour

Grease and line a 22.5 cm (9 in) round, loose-bottomed cake tin. In a saucepan, melt butter, then stir in crumbs. Mix, then press into tin.

Beat cheese, yogurt, egg yolks and 60 g (2 oz/¼ cup) sugar. Halve 5 passion fruit, scoop flesh into blender or food processor and process until seeds have come away. Strain juice into a stainless steel pan, add lemon juice and 30 g (1 oz/5 teaspoons) sugar. Bring to boil, then remove from the heat.

Sprinkle gelatine over 2 tablespoons water in a bowl and leave to soften. Stir into fruit juices. Cool; stir into cheese. Whisk egg whites with remaining sugar until firm. Fold into cheese, turn into tin and leave to set in the refrigerator for 2–3 hours.

To make topping, halve remaining passion fruit and scoop flesh and seeds into a stainless steel saucepan. Add orange juice and sugar and bring to boil. Mix cornflour with 3 tablespoons water, add to saucepan and simmer until thickened. Cool to room temperature, then pour over cheesecake. Leave to set.

Serves 8–10.

─── POLKADOT CHEESECAKE ───

1 quantity Plain Sponge Border, see page 10
90 g (3 oz/⅓ cup) butter
185 g (6 oz/1⅔ cups) semi-sweet biscuit crumbs
FILLING:
250 g (8 oz) Ricotta cheese
155 ml (5 fl oz/⅔ cup) thick sour cream
90 g (3 oz/⅓ cup) caster sugar
3 egg yolks
3 teaspoons powdered gelatine
155 ml (5 fl oz/⅔ cup) whipping cream
TOPPING:
3 egg whites
60 g (2 oz/¼ cup) caster sugar, plus extra for dusting
250 g (8 oz) redcurrants

Cut sponge border to reach 1 cm (½ in) above height of a 22.5 cm (9 in) round, loose-bottomed cake tin. Arrange sponge around sides of tin. Line base of tin with greaseproof paper. In a saucepan, melt butter, then stir in biscuit crumbs. Mix well, then press into base of cake tin.

In a bowl, beat cheese, sour cream, sugar and egg yolks until smooth. Sprinkle gelatine over 2 tablespoons water in a small bowl and leave to soften for 2–3 minutes. Stand the bowl in a saucepan of hot water and stir until dissolved and quite hot. Stir into cheese mixture.

Loosely whip cream and fold into cheese mixture with a large metal spoon. Turn into cake tin and leave to set in the refrigerator for 2–3 hours until set.

To make topping, whisk egg whites with sugar until standing in stiff peaks. Fold redcurrants into meringue and pile on top of cheese filling. Dust with caster sugar and brown under a medium grill.

Serves 6–8.

—POMEGRANATE CHEESECAKE

90 g (3 oz/⅓ cup) butter

185 g (6 oz/1⅓ cups) ginger biscuit crumbs

FILLING:

375 g (12 oz) Ricotta cheese

155 ml (5 fl oz/⅔ cup) natural yogurt

2 eggs, separated

90 g (3 oz/⅓ cup) caster sugar

pinch of ground cloves

2 small pomegranates

3 teaspoons powdered gelatine

finely grated peel and juice of 1 orange

TOPPING:

90 ml (3 fl oz/⅓ cup) grenadine syrup

6 teaspoons orange juice

6 teaspoons cornflour

155 ml (5 fl oz/⅔ cup) whipping cream

1 orange, sliced

Grease and line a 22.5 cm (9 in) round, loose-bottomed cake tin. In a pan, melt butter, stir in crumbs, then press into base of cake tin.

In a bowl, beat cheese, yogurt, egg yolks, 60 g (2 oz/¼ cup) sugar and cloves. Cut open one pomegranate and separate seeds. Add to cheese.

Sprinkle gelatine over orange juice in a small bowl and leave to soften for 2–3 minutes. Stand the bowl in a saucepan of hot water and stir until dissolved and quite hot. Stir into cheese with grated peel.

Whisk egg whites in a bowl with remaining sugar until firm, then fold into cheese. Turn into tin and leave to set for 2–3 hours.

To make topping, put grenadine and orange juice into a saucepan and bring to boil. Mix cornflour with 3 tablespoons water, stir into pan and simmer until thickened. Stir in remaining pomegranate seeds. Cool, pour over cheesecake and leave to set. Whip cream and pipe small rosettes around edge. Decorate with orange slices.

Serves 8–10.

– REFRIGERATOR CHEESECAKE –

90 g (3 oz/⅓ cup) butter

185 g (6 oz/1⅔ cups) semi-sweet biscuit crumbs

FILLING:

375 g (12 oz) full fat soft cheese

155 ml (5 fl oz/⅔ cup) thick sour cream

155 ml (5 fl oz/⅔ cup) natural yogurt

90 g (3 oz/⅓ cup) caster sugar

3 eggs, separated

4 teaspoons powdered gelatine

155 ml (5 fl oz/⅔ cup) whipping cream

TOPPING:

500 g (1 lb) assorted fresh fruits

30 g (1 oz) packet plain flan (cake) glaze, if desired

Grease and line a 20 cm (8 in) round, loose-bottomed cake tin. In a saucepan, melt butter, then stir in biscuit crumbs. Mix well, then press into base of cake tin.

In a bowl, beat cheese, sour cream, yogurt, 30 g (1 oz/5 tea-spoons) caster sugar and egg yolks until smooth.

Sprinkle gelatine over 2 table-spoons water in a small bowl and leave to soften for 2–3 minutes. Stand the bowl in a saucepan of hot water and stir until dissolved and quite hot. Stir into cheese.

Loosely whip cream in a bowl and fold into cheese. Whisk egg whites with remaining sugar until firm, then fold into cheese. Turn into cake tin and leave to set in the refrigerator for 2–3 hours.

To decorate, cut fruits into even-sized pieces and arrange over top of cheesecake. Make up flan glaze according to packet instructions and brush over the fruit if desired.

Serves 8–10.

— LEMON MERINGUE POSSET —

125 g (4 oz/½ cup) butter

250 g (8 oz/2¼ cups) digestive biscuit crumbs

FILLING·

3 egg yolks

470 ml (15 fl oz/1¾ cups) double(heavy) cream

juice of 2 lemons

90 g (3 oz/⅓ cup) caster sugar

TOPPING:

3 egg whites

30 g (1 oz/5 teaspoons) caster sugar, plus extra for sprinkling

lemon twist and sprig of mint

Grease and line a 20 cm (8 in) flan tin. In a saucepan, melt butter, then stir in biscuit crumbs. Mix well, then press into base and up sides of flan tin.

In a bowl, whisk egg yolks until pale in colour. Bring cream to the boil in a saucepan. Add lemon juice and sugar. Whisk into egg yolks, then spoon onto biscuit base. Leave to set in the refrigerator for 2–3 hours.

To make topping, whisk egg whites in a bowl with 30 g (1 oz/5 teaspoons) sugar until stiff, then pile onto the flan. Sprinkle with sugar and brown under a hot grill. Decorate with mint and lemon twist.

Serves 8–10.

MARSHMALLOW CHEESECAKE

90 g (3 oz/⅓ cup) butter
185 g (6 oz) round baby's rusks, crushed
FILLING:
375 g (12 oz) pink and white marsh-mallows, cut into small pieces
90 ml (3 fl oz/⅓ cup) milk
500 g (1 lb) low fat soft cheese
6 teaspoons lemon juice
250 ml (8 fl oz/1 cup) whipping cream
2–3 drops pink food colouring
TO DECORATE:
12 pink and white marshmallows
60 g (2 oz) plain (dark) chocolate, broken into pieces

Grease and line a 22.5 cm (9 in) round, loose-bottomed cake tin. In a saucepan, melt butter, then stir in crushed rusks. Mix well, then press into base of cake tin.

Put marshmallows into a saucepan with milk and melt over a low heat, stirring occasionally. Leave to cool.

In a bowl, beat cheese and lemon juice. Stir in marshmallow mixture and blend until smooth. In a separate bowl, whip cream, then fold into marshmallow mixture. Add food colouring. Spoon onto rusk base and leave to set in the refrigerator for 2–3 hours.

To decorate, halve marshmallows and arrange around edge of cheese-cake. Melt chocolate in the top of a double boiler or a bowl set over a saucepan of simmering water. Drizzle melted chocolate in centre of cheesecake.

Serves 8–10.

— STRAWBERRY CHEESECAKES —

60 g (2 oz/¼ cup) butter

125 g (4 oz/1¼ cups) digestive biscuit crumbs

FILLING:

250 g (8 oz) full fat soft cheese

315 ml (10 fl oz/1¼ cups) Greek style yogurt

2 egg yolks

90 g (3 oz/⅓ cup) caster sugar

3 teaspoons powdered gelatine

TOPPING:

500 g (1 lb) strawberries

155 ml (5 fl oz/⅔ cup) whipping cream

8 sprigs of mint

Place eight 8 cm (3½ in) muffin rings on a baking sheet and line with greaseproof paper. In a saucepan, melt butter, then stir in biscuit crumbs. Mix well, press into bottom of each ring, dividing mixture equally between them.

In a bowl, beat cheese and yogurt. Add egg yolks and sugar and beat until smooth.

Sprinkle gelatine over 2 tablespoons water in a small bowl and leave to soften for 2–3 minutes. Stand the bowl in a saucepan of hot water and stir until dissolved and quite hot. Stir into cheese mixture. Pour into muffin rings and leave to set in the refrigerator for 2–3 hours.

To decorate, slice strawberries and arrange over the cheesecakes. Whip cream and pipe a rosette of cream onto each cheesecake. Top each one with a sprig of mint.

Serves 8.

— BLACK CHERRY CHEESECAKE —

60 g (2 oz/¼ cup) butter
125 g (4 oz/1¼ cups) bran biscuit crumbs
FILLING:
500 g (1 lb) low fat soft cheese
155 ml (5fl oz/⅔ cup) Greek style yogurt
60 g (2 oz/¼ cup) caster sugar
grated peel and juice of 1 lemon
4 teaspoons powdered gelatine
1 egg white
TOPPING:
440 g (14 oz) can or jar stoned black cherries
2 tablespoons black cherry jam
sprig of mint

Grease and line a 19 x 8 cm (7½ x 3½ in) loaf tin. In a saucepan, melt butter, then stir in biscuit crumbs. Press into base of loaf tin.

In a bowl, beat cheese, yogurt, 30 g (1 oz/5 teaspoons) sugar, and lemon peel and juice until smooth.

Sprinkle gelatine over 2 table-spoons water in a small bowl and leave to soften for 2–3 minutes. Stand the bowl in a saucepan of hot water and stir until dissolved and quite hot. Stir into cheese mixture.

Whisk egg white in a bowl with remaining sugar until firm, then fold into cheese mixture with a large metal spoon. Turn into the loaf tin and leave to set in the refrigerator for 2–3 hours.

To make topping, drain cherries in a sieve. Warm jam in a saucepan without allowing to boil. Add cherries, then spread over top of cheesecake. Leave topping to cool before removing cheesecake from tin.

Cut into slices and decorate with a sprig of mint to serve.

Serves 6–8.

PEACH RASPBERRY CHEESECAKE

90 g (3 oz/⅓ cup) butter
155 g (5 oz/1⅓ cups) ginger biscuit crumbs
FILLING:
125 g (4 oz) full fat soft cheese
125 ml (4 fl oz/ ½ cup) Greek style yogurt
90 g (3 oz/⅓ cup) caster sugar
155 ml (5 fl oz/⅔ cup) whipping cream
4 teaspoons powdered gelatine
440 g (14 oz) can sliced peaches, roughly chopped
2 eggs
TO DECORATE:
375 g (12 oz) raspberries
155 ml (5 fl oz/⅔ cup) whipping cream
30 g (1 oz) toasted flaked almonds

Grease and line a 22.5 cm (9 in) round, loose-bottomed cake tin. In a saucepan, melt butter, then stir in biscuit crumbs. Mix well, then press into cake tin.

In a bowl, beat cheese, yogurt and 30 g (1 oz/5 teaspoons) sugar. Whip cream in a separate bowl and fold into cheese mixture.

Sprinkle gelatine over 2 tablespoons water in a small bowl and leave to soften for 2–3 minutes. Stand the bowl in a saucepan of hot water and stir until dissolved and quite hot. Stir into cheese mixture, then stir in chopped peaches.

Using a rotary or hand-held whisk, beat eggs and remaining sugar in a bowl until mixture is thick enough to hold trail of the whisk when beaters are lifted. Fold into cheese mixture. Turn into cake tin and leave to set in the refrigerator for 2–3 hours.

To decorate, arrange raspberries over surface, leaving a 2.5 cm (1 in) border around the edge. In a bowl, whip cream and pipe rosettes on the uncovered border. Decorate each rosette with 2 flaked almonds.

Serves 10.

- BLACKCURRANT CHEESECAKE -

60 g (2 oz/¼ cup) butter
125 g (4 oz/1¼ cups) digestive biscuit crumbs
FILLING:
500 g (1 lb) Ricotta cheese
100 g (3½ oz/⅓ cūp, plus 3 teaspoons) caster sugar
6 teaspoons lemon juice
2 eggs, separated
440 g (14 oz) blackcurrants, thawed if frozen
TOPPING:
155 ml (5 fl oz/⅔ cup) blackcurrant drink
6 teaspoons cornflour
TO DECORATE:
blackcurrant leaves or sprigs of mint

Preheat oven to 190C (375F/Gas 5). Grease and line a 22.5 cm (9 in) round, loose-bottomed cake tin. In a saucepan, melt butter, then stir in biscuit crumbs. Mix well, then press into base of cake tin.

In a bowl, beat cheese, 90 g (3 oz/⅓ cup) sugar, lemon juice and egg yolks until smooth. Stir in 125 g (4 oz) of the blackcurrants.

Whisk egg whites in a bowl with remaining sugar until firm. Fold egg whites into cheese mixture using a large metal spoon. Turn into cake tin and bake in the oven for 40 minutes.

To make topping, put blackcurrant drink into a small saucepan and bring to the boil. Mix cornflour with 4 tablespoons water and stir into pan. Simmer until thickened, then stir in remaining blackcurrants. Spread over top of cheesecake. Leave to cool before removing from cake tin.

Decorate with blackcurrant leaves or sprigs of mint.

Serves 8–10.

—— PINEAPPLE CHEESECAKE ——

60 g (2 oz/¼ cup) butter
125 g (4 oz/1¼ cups) digestive biscuit crumbs
pinch of ground cinnamon
FILLING:
375 g (12 oz) full fat soft cheese
2 eggs
125 g (4 oz/½ cup) caster sugar
2 teaspoons plain flour
few drops vanilla essence
TO DECORATE:
376 g (13¼ oz) can pineapple rings, drained and cut into pieces
440 g (14 oz) can red cherries
30 g (1 oz) piece angelica, cut into diamonds, or pineapple leaves
4 tablespoons apricot jam

Preheat oven to 180C (350F/Gas 4). Grease and line a 22.5 cm (9 in) round, loose-bottomed cake tin. In a saucepan, melt butter, then stir in biscuit crumbs and cinnamon. Mix well, then press into base of cake tin.

In a bowl, beat cheese, eggs, sugar, flour and vanilla essence until smooth. Turn into cake tin and bake in the oven for 45 minutes. Leave the cheesecake to cool before removing from tin.

To decorate, arrange the pineapple rings on top of the cheesecake and decorate with cherries and pieces of angelica or pineapple leaves. Melt jam in a saucepan with 1 tablespoon water and brush the fruit to glaze.

Serves 8.

— STRAWBERRY CHEESECAKE —

90 g (3 oz/⅓ cup) butter

125 g (4 oz/1¼ cups) rich tea biscuit crumbs

FILLING:

250 g (8 oz) Ricotta cheese

155 ml (5 fl oz/⅔ cup) natural yogurt

155 ml (5 fl oz/⅔ cup) thick sour cream

2 eggs, separated

finely grated peel and juice of 1 orange

500 g (1 lb) strawberries

5 teaspoons powdered gelatine

60 g (2 oz/¼ cup) caster sugar

TO DECORATE:

155 ml (5 fl oz/⅔ cup) whipping cream

Grease and line a 22.5 cm (9 in) round, loose-bottomed cake tin. In a saucepan, melt butter, then stir in biscuit crumbs. Mix well, then press into base of cake tin.

In a bowl, beat cheese, yogurt, sour cream, egg yolks, orange peel and juice. Reserve 10 strawberries for decoration. Blend remainder in a food processor or blender for 30 seconds or until puréed. Stir into cheese mixture.

Sprinkle gelatine over 2 table-spoons water in a small bowl and leave to soften for 2–3 minutes. Stand the bowl in a saucepan of hot water and stir until dissolved and quite hot. Stir into cheese mixture.

Whisk egg whites in a bowl with sugar until firm. Fold into straw-berry cheese with a large metal spoon. Turn into cake tin and leave in the refrigerator to set for 2–3 hours.

To decorate, whip cream and pipe a border of 20 rosettes around top edge of cheesecake. Halve reserved strawberries and top each rosette with a strawberry half.

Serves 8–10.

ORANGE CHEESECAKE

90 g (3 oz/⅓ cup) butter

125 g (4 oz) round baby's rusks, crushed

60 g (2 oz/¼ cup) caster sugar

FILLING:

750 g (1½ lb) medium fat curd cheese

finely grated peel and juice of 1 orange

2 eggs

60 g (2 oz/¼ cup) caster sugar

TOPPING:

440 g (14 oz) can mandarin orange segments

30 g (1 oz) packet orange flan (cake) glaze

mint leaves

Preheat oven to 190C (375F/Gas 5). Grease and line a 22.5 cm (9 in) round, loose-bottomed cake tin. In a saucepan, melt butter, then stir in rusks and sugar. Mix well, then press into base and up sides of cake tin.

In a bowl, beat cheese, orange peel and juice, eggs and sugar until smooth. Turn into cake tin and bake in the oven for 40 minutes. Leave to cool before removing from tin.

To decorate, drain mandarin oranges on absorbent kitchen paper, then arrange on the top of cheesecake.

Make up flan glaze according to packet instructions and brush over mandarin oranges. Decorate each orange with a mint leaf.

Serves 8–10.

—— RASPBERRY CHEESECAKE ——

1 quantity Chocolate Sponge Border, see page 11
60 g (2 oz/¼ cup) butter
125 g (4 oz/1¼ oz cups) digestive biscuit crumbs
FILLING:
250 g (8 oz) full fat soft cheese
155 ml (5 fl oz/⅔ cup) natural yogurt
155 ml (5 fl oz/⅔ cup) thick sour cream
2 eggs, separated
90 g (3 oz/⅓ cup) caster sugar
3 teaspoons powdered gelatine
TO DECORATE:
500 g (1 lb) raspberries
155 ml (5 fl oz/⅔ cup) whipping cream
60 g (2 oz) packet milk chocolate buttons

Arrange sponge border around sides of a 22.5 cm (9 in) round, loose-bottomed cake tin with side that was against greaseproof paper now against the tin. Line base of tin with greaseproof paper. In a saucepan, melt butter, then add biscuit crumbs.

Mix, then press into base of tin.

In a bowl, beat cheese, yogurt, sour cream, egg yolks and 60 g (2 oz/¼ cup) sugar until smooth.

Sprinkle gelatine over 2 table-spoons water in a small bowl and leave to soften for 2–3 minutes. Stand the bowl in a saucepan of hot water and stir until dissolved and quite hot. Stir into cheese mixture.

Whisk egg whites in a bowl with remaining sugar until firm. Fold into cheese. Turn into tin and leave to set in refrigerator 2–3 hours.

When cheesecake has set, remove from tin, then trim sponge border to 1 cm (½ in) above surface of cake. To decorate, arrange raspberries over cheesecake. Whip cream and pipe rosettes around edge of cheese-cake. Place raspberries and choco-late buttons on alternate rosettes.

Serves 8–10.

— GOOSEBERRY CHEESECAKE —

90 g (3 oz/⅓ cup) butter
125 g (4 oz/1¼ cups) digestive biscuit crumbs
30 g (1 oz/3 tablespoons) sunflower seeds
FILLING:
750 g (1½ lb) medium fat curd cheese
juice of 1 lemon
1 teaspoon orange flower water
2 eggs
60 g (2 oz/¼ cup) caster sugar
TOPPING:
440 g (14 oz) can gooseberries
6 teaspoons cornflour
TO SERVE:
cream or yogurt

Preheat oven to 190C (375F/Gas 5). Grease and line a 22.5 cm (9 in) round, loose-bottomed cake tin. In a saucepan, melt butter, then stir in biscuit crumbs and sunflower seeds. Mix well, then press into cake tin.

In a bowl, beat cheese, lemon juice, orange flower water, eggs and sugar. Turn into cake tin and bake in the oven for 40 minutes. Leave to cool.

Meanwhile, make topping. Drain gooseberries and put juice into a small saucepan. Bring to the boil. Mix cornflour with 4 tablespoons water. Stir into gooseberry juice and simmer to thicken. Add gooseberries, stir gently, then spread over cheese cake.

When cheesecake is cold, remove from tin and serve with cream or yogurt.

Serves 8–10.

LEMON CHEESECAKE

90 g (3 oz/⅓ cup) butter

185 g (6 oz/1⅔ cups) digestive biscuit crumbs

pinch of ground mace

FILLING:

250 g (8 oz) full fat soft cheese

250 ml (8 fl oz/1 cup) Greek style yogurt

2 eggs, separated

125 g (4 oz/½ cup) caster sugar

finely grated peel and juice of 2 lemons

4 teaspoons powdered gelatine

TOPPING:

6 teaspoons caster sugar

few drops yellow food colouring

2 teaspoons cornflour

125 g (4 oz) white marzipan

155 ml (5 fl oz/⅔ cup) whipping cream

small piece of angelica, cut into strips

Grease and line a 22.5 cm (9 in) round, loose-bottomed cake tin. In a pan, melt butter; stir in crumbs and mace. Mix, then press into tin.

In a bowl, beat cheese, yogurt, egg yolks, 60 g (2 oz/¼ cup) sugar, lemon peel and juice. Sprinkle gelatine over 2 tablespoons water in a small bowl and leave to soften for 2–3 minutes. Stand bowl in a pan of hot water and stir until dissolved.

Whisk egg whites in a bowl with remaining sugar until firm. Fold into cheese. Turn into tin and leave to set in refrigerator 2–3 hours.

To make topping, put sugar and 2 drops yellow colouring into a saucepan with 125 ml (4 fl oz/½ cup) water and bring to boil. Mix cornflour with 1 tablespoon water. Stir into pan; simmer to thicken. Cool slightly, pour over cake. Chill.

Colour marzipan with colouring. Divide into small balls and roll on a fine grater. Whip cream and pipe rosettes on cake. Decorate with 'lemons' and angelica.

Serves 8–10.

CRANBERRY CHEESECAKE

60 g (2 oz/¼ cup) butter
125 g (4 oz/1¼ cups) digestive biscuit crumbs
FILLING:
375 g (12 oz) cranberries, thawed if frozen
155 g (5 oz/⅔ cup) caster sugar
185 g (6 oz) full fat soft cheese
2 eggs, separated
3 teaspoons powdered gelatine
finely grated peel and juice of 1 orange
155 ml (5 fl oz/⅔ cup) whipping cream
TO DECORATE:
155 ml (5 fl oz/⅔ cup) whipping cream
30 g (1 oz) packet red or orange flan (cake) glaze, if desired

Grease and line a 22.5 cm (9 in) round, loose-bottomed cake tin. In a saucepan, melt butter, then stir in crumbs. Mix, then press into tin.

Put cranberries into a bowl with 60 g (2 oz/¼ cup) sugar and enough boiling water to cover. Leave to stand for 15 minutes until cooked.

In a bowl, beat cheese, remaining sugar and egg yolks. Sprinkle gelatine over 2 tablespoons water in a small bowl and leave to soften for 2–3 minutes. Stand the bowl in a saucepan of hot water and stir until dissolved. Stir into cheese mixture. Stir in 125 g (4 oz) of the cranberries and the orange peel and juice.

In a separate bowl, whip cream and fold into mixture with a large metal spoon. Whisk egg whites in a bowl until firm. Fold into cheese. Turn into tin and leave to set in the refrigerator for 2–3 hours.

To decorate, whip cream and pipe a border of cream around edge of cake. Arrange remaining cranberries in centre. Make up flan glaze according to packet instructions and brush over fruit to glaze, if desired.

Serves 8–10.

— REDCURRANT CHEESECAKE —

60 g (2 oz/¼ cup) butter

125 g (4 oz/1¼ cups) digestive biscuit crumbs

FILLING:

750 g (1½ lb) medium fat curd cheese

finely grated peel and juice of 1 lemon

2 eggs

60 g (2 oz/¼ cup) caster sugar

375 g (12 oz) redcurrants, thawed if frozen

TOPPING:

90 g (3 oz/¼ cup) redcurrant jelly

8–10 sprigs of mint

Preheat oven to 190C (375F/Gas 5). Grease and line a 22.5 cm (9 in) round, loose-bottomed cake tin. In a saucepan, melt butter, then stir in biscuit crumbs. Mix well, then press into cake tin.

In a bowl, beat cheese, lemon peel and juice, eggs and sugar. Stir 125 g (4 oz) of the redcurrants into cheese mixture. Turn into cake tin and bake in the oven for 45 minutes.

To make topping, melt redcurrant jelly in a saucepan. Stir in remaining redcurrants and spread over surface of cheesecake. Leave to cool before removing from tin. Decorate with sprigs of mint.

Serves 8–10.

—FIG & WALNUT CHEESECAKE—

60 g (2 oz/¼ cup) butter

125 g (4 oz/1¼ cups) digestive biscuit crumbs

60 g (2 oz/½ cup) ground walnuts

FILLING:

125 g (4 oz/¾ cup) dried figs

500 g (1 lb) Ricotta cheese

155 ml (5 fl oz/⅔ cup) whipping cream

2 eggs

30 g (1 oz/2 tablespoons) light soft brown sugar

3 teaspoons plain flour

TO DECORATE:

2 fresh figs

90 g (3 oz/1 cup) walnut halves

Prepare figs for filling. Put figs in a saucepan, cover with boiling water and simmer for 15 minutes. Leave to cool.

Meanwhile, preheat oven to 160C (325F/Gas 3). Grease and line a 20 cm (8 in) round, spring-form cake tin. In a saucepan, melt butter, then stir in biscuit crumbs and ground walnuts. Mix well, then press into base of cake tin.

In a bowl, beat cheese and cream until smooth. Add eggs, one at a time, then sugar. Roughly chop cooled figs and add to cheese mixture with flour. Turn into cake tin and bake in the oven for 1 hour 10 minutes. Leave to cool before removing from tin.

To decorate, trim top from fresh figs and cut into slices. Place fig slices around edge of cheesecake and arrange the walnut halves in centre.

Serves 8–10.

MAIDS OF HONOUR

1 quantity Sweet Shortcrust Pastry, see page 13

FILLING:

375 g (12 oz) medium fat curd cheese

3 egg yolks

60 g (2 oz/½ cup) ground almonds

60 g (2 oz/¼ cup) caster sugar

9 teaspoons milk

2 tablespoons currants

6 teaspoons apricot preserve

freshly grated nutmeg

Preheat oven to 190C (375F/Gas 5). Grease 24 individual tartlet tins. Roll out half the pastry at a time on a lightly floured surface and cut out 24 circles 4 cm (1½ in) bigger than the tins. Press circles into tins and prick several times with a fork. Refrigerate while preparing filling.

In a bowl, beat cheese, egg yolks, ground almonds and sugar until smooth. Add milk a little at a time, then stir in currants.

Spread ¼ teaspoon apricot preserve in the bottom of each pastry case. Spoon in filling, sprinkle with nutmeg and bake in the oven for 35 minutes or until golden.

Makes 24.

Note: Maids of Honour make a delicious tea time treat.

SULTANA CURD CAKE

1 quantity Sweet Shortcrust Pastry, see page 13

FILLING:

500 g (1 lb) medium fat curd cheese

315 ml (10 fl oz/1¼ cups) thick sour cream

2 eggs

90 g (3 oz/⅓ cup) light soft brown sugar

90 g (3 oz/⅓ cup) sultanas

3 teaspoons self-raising flour

TOPPING:

90 g (3 oz/3 cups) lightly crushed cornflakes

Grease and line a 20 cm (8 in) round, loose-bottomed cake tin. Roll out pastry on a lightly floured surface to a thickness of 0.5 cm (¼ in) and use to line base and 5 cm (2 in) up sides of tin. Refrigerate while preparing filling.

Meanwhile, preheat oven to 180C (350F/Gas 4) and make filling. In a bowl, beat cheese, sour cream, eggs and sugar until smooth. In a separate bowl, mix sultanas and flour until sultanas are evenly coated (this prevents them sinking during baking).

Stir the flour and sultanas into cheese mixture, then spoon into pastry case. Sprinkle cornflakes over top and bake in the oven for 45 minutes. Leave to cool before removing from tin.

Serves 8–10.

PRUNE & WALNUT CHEESECAKE

60 g (2 oz/¼ cup) butter
155 g (5 oz/1⅓ cups) semi-sweet biscuit crumbs
30 g (1 oz/¼ cup) ground walnuts
FILLING:
500 g (1 lb) Ricotta cheese
155 ml (5 fl oz/⅔ cup) thick sour cream
2 eggs
60 g (2 oz/¼ cup) light soft brown sugar
440 g (14 oz) can prunes
90 g (3 oz/¾ cup) chopped walnuts
3 teaspoons plain flour
TO DECORATE:
10 dried prunes
6 teaspoons milk
90 g (3 oz) full fat soft cheese
6 teaspoons icing sugar
90 g (3 oz/¾ cup) chopped walnuts
3 teaspoons clear honey

Preheat oven to 160C (325F/Gas 3). Grease and line a 20 cm (8 in) round, spring-form cake tin. In a saucepan, melt butter, then stir in crumbs and ground walnuts. Mix well, then press into base of tin.

To make filling, beat Ricotta cheese, sour cream, eggs and sugar in a bowl until smooth. Drain canned prunes, discard stones and blend flesh to a purée in a blender or food processor. Add purée to cheese mixture with walnuts and flour. Turn into tin and bake in the oven for 50 minutes. Cool in tin.

To decorate, put dried prunes into a pan, cover with boiling water and simmer for 15 minutes. Cool. In a bowl, blend milk into cheese to form piping consistency. Add icing sugar. Pipe 10 rosettes around cheesecake.

Mix chopped walnuts and honey. Remove stones from prunes and stuff with walnut mixture. Place a stuffed prune on each rosette.

Serves 8-10.

—— POPPY SEED CHEESECAKE ——

60 g (2 oz/¼ cup) butter
185g (6 oz/1 cup) bulgar wheat
3 teaspoons clear honey

FILLING:
500 g (1 lb) Ricotta cheese
60 ml (2 fl oz/¼ cup) whipping cream
3 egg yolks
3 teaspoons plain flour
1 teaspoon ground cinnamon
6 teaspoons poppy seeds
9 teaspoons clear honey

TOPPING:
60 g (2 oz/¼ cup) butter
90 g (3 oz/¾ cup) poppy seeds
6 teaspoons caster sugar
3 teaspoons plain flour

Preheat oven to 180C (350F/Gas 4). Grease and line a 20 cm (8 in)

round, loose-bottomed cake tin. In a saucepan, melt butter, then stir in bulgar wheat and honey. Mix well, then press into cake tin.

In a bowl, beat cheese, cream, egg yolks and flour. Add cinnamon, poppy seeds and honey and beat until smooth. Turn into cake tin and bake in the oven for 30 minutes.

To make topping, melt butter in a saucepan and stir in poppy seeds and sugar, then flour. Spread over surface of cheesecake and return to the oven for a further 25 minutes until a skewer inserted into cake comes away clean. Leave to cool before removing from cake tin.

Serves 10–12.

—— COFFEE NUT CHEESECAKE ——

60 g (2 oz/¼ cup) butter

155 g (5 oz/1⅓ cups) semi-sweet biscuit crumbs

30 g (1 oz/¼ cup) ground walnuts

FILLING:

500 g (1 lb) medium fat soft cheese

315 ml (10 fl oz/1¼ cups) thick sour cream

90 g (3 oz/⅓ cup) light soft brown sugar

2 eggs

60 g (2 oz/½ cup) roughly chopped walnuts

6 teaspoons instant coffee granules

9 teaspoons boiling water

TO DECORATE:

155 ml (5 fl oz/⅔ cup) whipping cream

60 g (2 oz/⅔ cup) walnut halves

20 chocolate coffee beans

Preheat oven to 180C (350F/Gas 4). Grease and line a 20 cm (8 in) round, spring-form cake tin. In a saucepan, melt butter, then stir in biscuit crumbs and ground walnuts. Mix well, then press into base of cake tin.

In a bowl, beat cheese, sour cream, sugar and eggs until smooth. Stir in chopped walnuts. Put coffee granules into a small bowl, add boiling water and stir until dissolved. Blend into cheese mixture. Turn into cake tin and bake in the oven for 45 minutes. Leave to cool before removing from tin.

To decorate, whip cream in a bowl, then pipe a border of cream around edge of cheesecake and decorate with walnut halves and chocolate coffee beans.

Serves 8–10.

FLAPJACK CHEESECAKE

60 g (2 oz/¼ cup) butter
1 tablespoon golden syrup
30 g (1 oz/5 teaspoons) soft brown sugar
90 g (3 oz/⅔ cup) jumbo oats
30 g (1 oz/3 tablespoons) sunflower seeds
1 tablespoon flaked almonds
1 tablespoon bran fibre
FILLING:
500 g (1 lb) medium fat curd cheese
2 eggs
60 g (2 oz/¼ cup) caster sugar
few drops vanilla essence
3 teaspoons plain flour
TOPPING:
60 g (2 oz/⅓ cup) malted rolled oats

Preheat oven to 190C (375F/Gas 5). Grease and line a 22.5 cm (9 in) round, loose-bottomed cake tin. In a saucepan, melt butter, then stir in syrup and sugar and heat without bringing to boil.

Remove saucepan from heat and stir in jumbo oats, sunflower seeds, flaked almonds and bran fibre. Mix well, then press into base of cake tin.

In a bowl, beat cheese, eggs, sugar, vanilla essence and flour until smooth. Turn into cake tin and sprinkle malted rolled oats over top. Bake in the oven for 40 minutes. Leave the cheesecake to cool before removing from tin.

Serves 8–10.

CHEESECAKE FINGERS

1 quantity Cheesecake Pastry, see
page 12

FILLING:

500 g (1 lb) medium fat curd cheese

155 ml (5 fl oz/⅔ cup) thick sour cream

2 eggs

125 g (4 oz/½ cup) caster sugar

6 teaspoons semolina

30 g (1 oz/¼ cup) sultanas

30 g (1 oz/¼ cup) raisins

30 g (1 oz/¼ cup) roughly chopped glacé
cherries

30 g (1 oz/¼ cup) mixed citrus peel

3 teaspoons plain flour

finely grated peel and juice of 1 orange

TO GLAZE:

2 tablespoons apricot preserve

Preheat oven to 160C (325F/Gas 3). Grease and line a 22.5 cm (9 in) square, 4 cm (1½ in) deep, tin. Roll out pastry on a lightly floured surface to a thickness of 0.5 cm (¼ in) and use to line base of tin. Refrigerate while making filling.

In a bowl, beat cheese, sour cream, eggs, sugar and semolina until smooth. Put all dried fruit into a bowl and sprinkle flour over top (this prevents fruit sinking during baking). Stir fruit and flour into cheese mixture with orange peel and juice. Turn into cake tin and bake in the oven for 1 hour until a skewer inserted into cake comes away clean.

To glaze, put apricot preserve into a small saucepan with 1 table-spoon water. Bring to boil, then brush thinly over surface of cheese-cake. Leave to cool before cutting into fingers.

Makes 12.

— WINE & GRAPE CHEESECAKE —

90 g (3 oz/⅓ cup) butter

185 g (6 oz/1⅔ cups) semi-sweet biscuit crumbs

FILLING:

375 g (12 oz) full fat soft cheese

2 eggs

30 g (1 oz/5 teaspoons) caster sugar

155 ml (5 fl oz/⅔ cup) thick sour cream

6 teaspoons plain flour

155 ml (5 fl oz/⅔ cup) dry white wine

500 g (1 lb) large green grapes

Preheat oven to 180C (350F/Gas 4). Grease and line a 22.5 cm (9 in) round, loose-bottomed cake tin. In a saucepan, melt butter, then stir in biscuit crumbs. Mix well, then press into base of cake tin.

In a bowl, beat cheese, eggs and sugar. Add sour cream and flour, then gradually beat in wine until mixture is smooth.

Remove pips from 185 g (6 oz) of the green grapes. Peel the grapes and stir whole grapes into cheese mixture. Turn into cake tin and bake in the oven for 50 minutes.

To decorate, cut remaining grapes in half and remove pips. Arrange grapes, cut side down, on top of cheesecake, starting from the outside and working in towards the centre.

Serves 8–10.

—— LIQUEUR CHEESECAKE ——

90 g (3 oz/⅓ cup) butter

185 g (6 oz/1⅔ cups) digestive biscuit crumbs

FILLING:

500 g (1 lb) Ricotta cheese

155 ml (5 fl oz/⅔ cup) thick sour cream

3 eggs

3 teaspoons plain flour

90 g (3 oz/⅓ cup) soft brown sugar

finely grated peel and juice of 2 oranges

75 ml (2½ fl oz/⅓ cup) Grand Marnier

TO DECORATE:

3 small oranges

155 ml (5 fl oz/⅔ cup) whipping cream

250 g (8 oz) strawberries

Preheat oven to 180C (350F/Gas 4). Grease and line a 22.5 cm (9 in) round, spring-form cake tin. In a saucepan, melt butter, then stir in biscuit crumbs. Mix well, then press into base of cake tin.

In a bowl, beat cheese, sour cream, eggs, flour and sugar. Add orange peel and juice and Grand Marnier and beat until smooth. Turn into cake tin and bake in the oven for 50 minutes. Leave to cool before removing from the tin.

To decorate, cut oranges into 0.5 cm (¼ in) slices. Make a cut from centre to edge of each slice, then hold slice at each side of cut and twist to form an S shape. Arrange orange twists around edge of cheese-cake.

Whip cream in a bowl, then pipe a rosette of cream into each orange twist and add a strawberry.

Serves 8–10.

—— CAMPARI CHEESECAKE ——

90 g (3 oz/⅓ cup) butter	
185 g (6 oz/1⅔ cups) plain biscuit crumbs	
FILLING:	
250 g (8 oz) low fat soft cheese	
155 ml (5 fl oz/⅔ cup) natural yogurt	
155 ml (5 fl oz/⅔ cup) whipping cream	
finely grated peel and juice of 1 pink grapefruit	
75 ml (2½ fl oz/⅓ cup) Campari	
4 teaspoons powdered gelatine	
2 eggs	
60 g (2 oz/¼ cup) caster sugar	
TO DECORATE:	
2 kiwi fruit	
2 pink grapefruit, peeled and divided into segments	
5 maraschino cherries, halved	

Grease and line a 20 cm (8 in) round, loose-bottomed cake tin. In a saucepan, melt butter, then stir in biscuit crumbs. Mix well, then press into base of cake tin.

In a bowl, beat cheese, yogurt and cream until smooth. Add grapefruit peel and juice and Campari and beat until smooth.

Sprinkle gelatine over 2 tablespoons water in a small bowl and leave to soften for 2–3 minutes. Stand bowl in a saucepan of hot water and stir until dissolved. Stir into cheese mixture.

Using a rotary or hand-held whisk, beat eggs and sugar in a bowl until mixture is thick enough to hold trail of the whisk when beaters are lifted. Fold beaten eggs into cheese mixture, then turn into cake tin. Leave to set in the refrigerator for 2–3 hours.

To decorate, slice kiwi fruit. Turn out cheesecake and arrange segments of grapefruit, slices of kiwi fruit and maraschino cherries around the edge.

Serves 8–10.

——PEAR & WINE CHEESECAKE——

1 quantity Cheesecake Pastry, see page 12

FILLING:

375 g (12 oz) full fat soft cheese

2 eggs

90 g (3 oz/⅓ cup) caster sugar

155 ml (5 fl oz/⅔ cup) natural yogurt

6 teaspoons lemon juice

½ teaspoon ground cinnamon

pinch of ground cloves

3 teaspoons plain flour

TOPPING:

5 small pears

625 ml (20 fl oz/2½ cups) red wine

185 g (6 oz/¾ cup) granulated sugar

½ teaspoon red food colouring

Prepare pears for topping. Peel pears. Put wine, granulated sugar and food colouring into a large saucepan with 315 ml (10 fl oz/1¼ cups) water and bring to the boil. Add pears and simmer for 25 minutes. Allow to cool in the syrup.

Meanwhile, grease a 22.5 cm (9 in) round, loose-bottomed cake tin. Preheat oven to 180C (350F/Gas 4). Roll out pastry on a lightly floured surface to a thickness of 0.5 cm (¼ in) and use to line base of tin. Refrigerate while preparing filling.

To make filling, beat cheese, eggs, caster sugar and yogurt in a bowl. Add lemon juice, cinnamon, cloves and flour and beat until smooth.

Cut 2 of the pears into 1 cm (½ in) dice and stir into cheese mixture. Turn into cake tin and bake in the oven for 50 minutes. Cool in tin.

To decorate, slice remaining pears lengthwise and arrange in a fan shape over surface of the cheesecake.

Serves 8–10.

— RUM & RAISIN CHEESECAKE —

60 g (2 oz/¼ cup) butter
125 g (4 oz/1¼ cups) sweetmeal biscuit crumbs
FILLING:
125 g (4 oz/½ cup) large raisins
90 ml (3 fl oz/⅓ cup) dark rum
375 g (12 oz) medium fat curd cheese
155 ml (5 fl oz/⅔ cup) whipping cream
2 eggs
60 g (2 oz/¼ cup) soft brown sugar
few drops vanilla essence

Put raisins for filling into a small bowl and pour over the rum. Leave to soak while preparing biscuit base.

Preheat oven to 180C (350F/Gas 4). Grease and line a 20 cm (8 in) round, loose-bottomed cake tin. In a saucepan, melt butter, then stir in biscuit crumbs. Mix well, then press into base of cake tin.

In a bowl, beat cheese, cream and eggs until smooth. Add sugar, vanilla essence, raisins and rum and blend until smooth. Turn into cake tin and bake in the oven for 50 minutes. Leave to cool before removing from tin. This cheesecake is best eaten 2 days after baking.

Serves 8–10.

— TUTTI FRUTTI CHEESECAKE —

packet of 8 trifle sponges
FILLING:
375 g (12 oz) full fat soft cheese
60 g (2 oz/¼ cup) caster sugar
2 eggs
3 teaspoons powdered gelatine
30 g (1 oz/¼ cup) flaked almonds
30 g (1 oz/¼ cup) chopped mixed citrus peel
30 g (1 oz/¼ cup) chopped raisins
9 teaspoons Grand Marnier
30 g (1 oz/¼ cup) chopped glacé cherries
TO DECORATE:
5 glacé cherries, halved
30 g (1 oz) angelica, cut into small strips

Grease and line a 20 x 10 cm (8 x 4 in) loaf tin. To make filling, beat cheese, sugar and eggs in a bowl until light and fluffy.

Sprinkle gelatine over 2 tablespoons water in a small bowl and leave to soften for 2–3 minutes. Stand the bowl in a saucepan of hot water and stir until dissolved and quite hot. Stir into cheese mixture.

Stir in flaked almonds, mixed citrus peel, raisins, Grand Marnier and glacé cherries. Turn into cake tin.

Cut trifle sponges to fit the tin and arrange on top of the filling. Leave to set in the refrigerator for 2–3 hours.

To decorate, turn out cheesecake onto a serving dish and decorate the top with halved glacé cherries and angelica.

Serves 10.

TIPSY CHEESECAKE

90 g (3 oz/⅓ cup) butter
185 g (6 oz/1⅔ cups) plain biscuit crumbs
FILLING:
60 g (2 oz) macaroons
75 ml (2½ fl oz/⅓ cup) dry sherry
375 g (12 oz) medium fat curd cheese
155 ml (5 fl oz/⅔ cup) whipping cream
2 eggs
90 g (3 oz/⅓ cup) caster sugar
500 g (1 lb) raspberries
30 g (1 oz/2 tablespoons) icing sugar

Put the macaroons for the filling into a small bowl. Pour over the sherry and leave to soak for 15–20 minutes until sherry is absorbed.

Meanwhile, preheat oven to 180C (350F/Gas 4). Grease and line a 20 cm (8 in) round, loose-bottomed cake tin. In a saucepan, melt butter, then stir in biscuit crumbs. Mix well, then press into base of cake tin.

In a bowl, beat cheese, cream, eggs and caster sugar until smooth (do not overbeat or cheesecake will rise too much during baking).

Stir macaroons into mixture, trying not to break them up. Stir in 185 g (6 oz) of the raspberries. Turn into cake tin and bake in the oven for 50 minutes. Leave to cool before removing from tin.

To decorate, dust surface of cheesecake with icing sugar and arrange remaining raspberries around edge in 3 rows.

Serves 6–8.

PERNOD CHEESECAKE

60 g (2 oz/¼ cup) butter
125 g (4 oz/1¼ cups) digestive biscuit crumbs
FILLING:
220 g (7 oz) medium fat soft cheese
155 ml (5 fl oz/⅔ cup) natural yogurt
155 ml (5 fl oz/⅔ cup) whipping cream
6 teaspoons Pernod
4 teaspoons powdered gelatine
2 eggs
2 tablespoons clear honey
finely grated peel of 1 orange
TO DECORATE:
3 kiwi fruit
155 ml (5 fl oz/⅔ cup) whipping cream
60 g (2 oz) packet milk chocolate buttons

Grease and line a 22.5 cm (9 in) round, loose-bottomed cake tin. In a saucepan, melt butter, then stir in biscuit crumbs. Mix well, then press into base of cake tin.

In a bowl, beat cheese and yogurt. Whip cream in a separate bowl, then fold into cheese with Pernod.

Sprinkle gelatine over 3 tablespoons cold water and leave to soften for 2–3 minutes. Stand the bowl in a saucepan of hot water and stir until dissolved. Stir into cheese mixture.

Using a rotary or hand-held whisk, beat eggs, honey and orange peel in a bowl until mixture is thick enough to hold trail of the whisk when beaters are lifted. Fold into cheese mixture, then turn into cake tin. Leave to set in refrigerator for 2–3 hours before removing from tin.

To decorate, peel kiwi fruit, halve them lengthwise and cut into half moon-shaped slices. Whip cream and pipe rosettes of cream around edge of cheesecake. Arrange kiwi fruit slices and chocolate buttons between the rosettes.

Serves 8–10.

——PINA COLADA CHEESECAKE-- -

90 g (3 oz/⅓ cup) butter
185 g (6 oz/1⅓ cups) plain biscuit crumbs
FILLING:
375 g (12 oz) full fat soft cheese
155 ml (5 fl oz/⅔ cup) thick sour cream
155 ml (5 fl oz/⅔ cup) natural yogurt
2 eggs
90 g (3 oz/⅓ cup) caster sugar
3 teaspoons plain flour
2 tablespoons creamed coconut
75 ml (2½ fl oz/⅓ cup) light rum
440 g (14 oz) can pineapple rings
4 maraschino cherries, roughly chopped
TOPPING:
60 g (2 oz/¼ cup) caster sugar
2 egg whites
3 tablespoons desiccated coconut
5 maraschino cherries

Preheat oven to 180C (350F/Gas 4). Grease and line a 22.5 cm (9 in) round, spring-form cake tin. In a saucepan, melt butter, then stir in biscuit crumbs. Mix well, then press into base of cake tin.

In a bowl, beat cheese, sour cream, yogurt and eggs until smooth. Beat in sugar and flour. Soften creamed coconut in the rum, then stir into cheese mixture. Cut 3 of pineapple rings into even-sized pieces and stir into mixture with chopped cherries. Turn into cake tin and bake in the oven for 45 minutes.

To make topping, set aside 1–2 teaspoons sugar. Whisk remaining sugar and egg whites in a bowl until stiff. Fold in desiccated coconut with a large metal spoon, then pile mixture onto cheesecake. Cut remaining pineapple into wedges and dot them over the surface with the cherries. Sprinkle with reserved sugar and return to the oven until brown on top.

Serves 8–10.

WHISKY CHEESECAKE

90 g (3 oz/⅓ cup) butter
185 g (6 oz/1⅔ cups) ginger biscuit crumbs
FILLING:
500 g (1 lb) full fat soft cheese
155 ml (5 fl oz/⅔ cup) thick sour cream
2 eggs
90 g (3 oz/⅓ cup) soft brown sugar
3 teaspoons plain flour
finely grated peel and juice of 1 orange
30 g (1 oz) stem ginger, chopped
75 ml (2½ fl oz/⅓ cup) whisky
TO DECORATE:
60 g (2 oz) stem ginger
1 orange

Preheat oven to 180C (350F/Gas 4). Grease and line a 20 cm (8 in) round, spring-form cake tin. In a saucepan, melt butter, then stir in biscuit crumbs. Mix well, then press into base of cake tin.

In a bowl, beat cheese, sour cream and eggs until smooth. Add sugar, flour, orange peel and juice. Stir in chopped ginger and whisky. Turn into cake tin and bake in the oven for 50 minutes. Leave to cool before releasing cake tin.

To decorate, slice stem ginger into thin rounds and arrange around edge of cheesecake. Remove outer peel of orange with a vegetable peeler and simmer in a small saucepan of boiling water for 3–4 minutes until soft. Cut into thin strips and wind each strip around a chopstick. Remove from the chopstick and arrange on the ginger slices.

Serves 8–10.

—— MERINGUE CHEESECAKE ——

90 g (3 oz/⅓ cup) butter

185 g (6 oz/1⅔ cups) ginger biscuit crumbs

FILLING:

750 g (1½ lb) full fat soft cheese

60 g (2 oz/¼ cup) soft brown sugar

3 eggs

finely grated peel and juice of 1 orange

few drops vanilla essence

155 ml (5 fl oz/⅔ cup) whipping cream

220 g (7 oz) plain (dark) chocolate, broken into pieces

MERINGUE TOPPING:

3 egg whites

155 g (5 oz/⅔ cup) caster sugar

6 teaspoons cocoa powder

155 ml (5 fl oz/⅔ cup) whipping cream

icing sugar for dusting

Make meringue for topping. Preheat oven to 150C (300F/Gas 2). Line 2 baking sheets with non-stick parchment. In a bowl, whisk egg whites with 30 g (1 oz/5 teaspoons) sugar until firm. Repeat until all sugar is added. Sift cocoa over and fold in.

Spoon into a piping bag fitted with a 1 cm (½ in) nozzle and pipe lengths of meringue onto baking sheets. Bake in oven with door slightly ajar for 1½–2 hours. Remove from oven and increase oven temperature to 190C (375F/Gas 5).

Grease and line a 22.5 cm (9 in) round, loose-bottomed cake tin. In a pan, melt butter, then stir in crumbs. Mix well; press into base of tin.

To make filling, beat cheese, sugar, eggs, orange peel and juice and essence in a bowl. Bring cream to boil in a pan. Remove from heat, add chocolate and stir until melted. Blend into cheese. Turn into tin and bake 50 minutes. Cool in tin.

To finish topping, whip cream and spread over. Top with meringue pieces. Dust with icing sugar.

Serves 8–10.

─── WHITE CHOCOLATE CAKE ───

60 g (2 oz/¼ cup) butter
125 g (4 oz/1¼ cups) chocolate digestive biscuit crumbs

FILLING:
375 g (12 oz) Ricotta cheese
185 g (6 oz/1 cup) sweet chestnut purée
155 ml (5 fl oz/⅔ cup) whipping cream
125 g (4 oz) white chocolate, broken into pieces
6 teaspoons cognac
3 eggs
3 teaspoons plain flour

TO DECORATE:
125 g (4 oz) white chocolate
155 ml (5 fl oz/⅔ cup) whipping cream
10 pieces candied chestnut
caster sugar
10 angelica 'leaves'

Preheat oven to 180C (350F/Gas 4). Grease and line a 20 cm (8 in) round, loose-bottomed cake tin. In a saucepan, melt butter, then stir in biscuit crumbs. Mix well and press into base of cake tin.

In a bowl, beat cheese and chestnut purée. Bring cream to the boil in a small saucepan. Remove from heat, add chocolate and stir until melted. Add cognac and stir into cheese mixture. Add eggs and flour and beat well. Turn into cake tin and bake in the oven for 1 hour. Leave to cool before removing from tin.

To decorate, grate white chocolate over surface of cheesecake. Whip cream and pipe a border of 10 large rosettes around edge and decorate with pieces of candied chestnut rolled in caster sugar and topped with angelica 'leaves'.

Serves 10–12.

- CHOC & WHISKY CHEESECAKE -

60 g (2 oz/¼ cup) butter

185 g (6 oz/1⅔ cups) ginger biscuit crumbs

FILLING:

750 g (1½ lb) full fat soft cheese

60 g (2 oz/¼ cup) soft brown sugar

2 eggs

6 teaspoons cocoa powder

2 teaspoons ground ginger

155 ml (5 fl oz/⅔ cup) whipping cream

250 g (8 oz) plain (dark) chocolate, broken into pieces

90 ml (3 fl oz/⅓ cup) whisky

TO DECORATE:

6 teaspoons cocoa powder

4 teaspoons icing sugar

½ teaspoon ground ginger

Preheat oven to 180C (350F/Gas 4). Grease and line a 20 cm (8 in) round, loose-bottomed cake tin. In a saucepan, melt butter, then stir in biscuit crumbs. Mix well, then press into base of cake tin.

To make filling, beat together cheese, brown sugar and eggs in a bowl. Sift in cocoa powder and ginger and beat until smooth. Bring cream to boil in a small saucepan. Remove from heat, add chocolate and stir until melted. Stir in whisky and blend into cheese mixture.

Turn into cake tin and bake in the oven for 45 minutes. Leave to cool before removing from cake tin.

To decorate, cut out 5 strips of greaseproof paper 2 cm (¾ in) wide and lay them at intervals over surface of cheesecake. Mix together cocoa powder, icing sugar and ground ginger, then sift over cake. Carefully remove strips and serve at once.

Serves 8-10.

KUMQUAT CHOC CHEESECAKE

90 g (3 oz/⅓ cup) butter
250 g (8 oz/2¼ cups) ginger biscuit crumbs
FILLING:
750 g (1½ lb) Ricotta cheese
60 g (2 oz/¼ cup) dark soft brown sugar
3 eggs
finely grated peel and juice of 1 orange
1 teaspoon orange flower water, if desired
155 ml (5 fl oz/⅔ cup) whipping cream
220 g (7 oz) plain (dark) chocolate, broken into pieces
TOPPING:
125 g (4 oz) kumquats
125 g (4 oz) chocolate flake bar

Preheat oven to 180C (350F/Gas 4). Grease and line a 20 cm (8 in) round, loose-bottomed cake tin. In a saucepan, melt butter, then stir in biscuit crumbs. Mix well, then press into base of cake tin.

In a bowl, beat cheese, sugar and eggs. Stir in orange peel and juice and orange flower water, if desired. Bring cream to the boil in a small saucepan. Remove from heat, add chocolate and stir until melted.

Add chocolate and cream to cheese mixture and beat until smooth. Turn into cake tin and bake in the oven for 45 minutes. Leave to cool before removing cheesecake from tin.

To decorate, slice kumquats thinly and arrange around edge of cheese-cake so that slices overlap. Flake chocolate over surface and chill before serving.

Serves 8–10.

— CHOC PECAN CHEESECAKE —

60 g (2 oz/¼ cup) butter
125 g (4 oz/1¼ cups) semi-sweet biscuit crumbs
FILLING:
750 g (1½ lb) Ricotta cheese
2 tablespoons maple syrup
2 eggs
155 ml (5 fl oz/⅔ cup) whipping cream
220 g (7 oz) plain (dark) chocolate, broken into pieces
90 g (3 oz/¾ cup) chopped pecan nuts
TOPPING:
90 g (3 oz/¾ cup) pecan nuts
90 g (3 oz) plain (dark) chocolate, grated
2 tablespoons icing sugar

Preheat oven to 180C (350F/Gas 4). Grease and line a 20 cm (8 in) round, loose-bottomed cake tin. In a saucepan, melt butter, then stir in biscuit crumbs. Mix well, then press into base of cake tin.

In a bowl, beat cheese, maple syrup and eggs until smooth. Bring cream to the boil in a small saucepan. Remove from heat, add chocolate and stir until melted. Blend into cheese mixture, then add chopped pecan nuts.

Turn into cake tin and bake in the oven for 45 minutes. Leave to cool before removing from tin.

To decorate, arrange pecan nuts around edge of cake. Sprinkle grated chocolate in centre and dust with icing sugar.

Serves 8–10.

RICH CHOCOLATE CHEESECAKE

90 g (3 oz/⅓ cup) butter

185 g (6 oz/1⅔ cups) chocolate digestive biscuit crumbs

FILLING:

750 g (1½ lb) full fat soft cheese

3 eggs

60 g (2 oz/¼ cup) dark soft brown sugar

3 tablespoons molasses or black treacle

6 teaspoons cocoa powder

1 teaspoon ground allspice

finely grated peel and juice of 1 orange

155 ml (5 fl oz/⅔ cup) whipping cream

250 g (8 oz) plain (dark) chocolate, broken into pieces

60 g (2 oz/¼ cup) soft unsalted butter

TOPPING:

250 g (8 oz) plain (dark) chocolate, flaked

125 g (4 oz) white chocolate, flaked

Preheat oven to 180C (350F/Gas 4). Grease and line a 22.5 cm (9 in) round, loose-bottomed cake tin. In a saucepan, melt butter, then stir in crumbs. Mix, then press into tin.

In a bowl, beat cheese, eggs, sugar, molasses or black treacle, cocoa powder, allspice, orange peel and juice. Bring cream to the boil in a small saucepan. Remove from the heat, add chocolate and stir until melted. Beat in butter, then blend into cheese mixture.

Turn into cake tin and bake in the oven for 50 minutes. Leave to cool before removing from tin.

To decorate, arrange plain (dark) chocolate flakes in overlapping layers around edge of cake, alternating with the 2 coloured chocolates towards the centre.

Serves 10–12.

—— FUDGENUT CHEESECAKE ——

60 g (2 oz/¼ cup) butter

125 g (4 oz/1¼ cups) ginger biscuit crumbs

FILLING:

750 g (1½ lb) full fat soft cheese

60 g (2 oz/¼ cup) dark soft brown sugar

3 eggs

155 ml (5 fl oz/⅔ cup) whipping cream

220 g (7 oz) plain (dark) chocolate, broken into pieces

60 g (2 oz/½ cup) mixed chopped nuts

60 g (2 oz/⅓ cup) chopped raisins

TO DECORATE:

6 teaspoons icing sugar

Preheat oven to 180C (350F/Gas 4). Grease and line a 22.5 cm (9 in) round, loose-bottomed cake tin. In a saucepan, melt butter, then stir in biscuit crumbs. Mix well, then press into base of cake tin.

In a bowl, beat cheese, sugar and eggs. Bring cream to the boil in a small saucepan. Remove from the heat, add chocolate and stir until melted. Blend into cheese mixture and add chopped nuts and raisins. Turn into cake tin and bake in the oven for 50 minutes. Leave to cool before removing from the tin.

To decorate, dust top of cheesecake with icing sugar.

Serves 10–12.

— CHOC & ORANGE TERRINE —

½ quantity Cheesecake Pastry, see page 12

FILLING:

375 g (12 oz) Ricotta cheese

30 g (1 oz/5 teaspoons) soft brown sugar

1 egg

finely grated peel and juice of 1 orange

155 ml (5 fl oz/⅔ cup) whipping cream

185 g (6 oz) plain (dark) chocolate, broken into pieces

TO DECORATE:

6 teaspoons cocoa powder, if desired

3 teaspoons icing sugar, if desired

90 g (3 oz) marzipan

3–4 drops orange food colouring

8 cloves

155 ml (5 fl oz/⅔ cup) whipping cream

Preheat oven to 180C (350F/Gas 4). Line a 20 x 10 cm (8 x 4 in) loaf tin with greaseproof paper.

To make filling, beat cheese, sugar, egg, orange peel and juice in a bowl. Bring cream to the boil in a small saucepan. Remove from the heat, add chocolate and stir until melted. Blend into cheese mixture. Pour into loaf tin and bake in oven for 20 minutes.

Meanwhile, roll out pastry on a lightly floured surface to a rectangle same size as top of loaf tin. Lay pastry over partially-cooked cheesecake and bake for a further 20 minutes until pastry is cooked. Leave to cool before turning out.

To decorate, mix cocoa powder and icing sugar together and dust over terrine, if desired. Colour marzipan with orange colouring and shape into balls the size of a hazelnut. Roll them on a fine cheese grater. Push a clove into top of each marzipan 'orange'. Whip cream and pipe rosettes on cheesecake. Arrange 'oranges' on top.

Serves 6–8.

– CHOC & HONEY CHEESECAKE –

90 g (3 oz/⅓ cup) butter

185 g (6 oz/1⅔ cups) digestive biscuit crumbs

FILLING:

750 g (1½ lb) Ricotta cheese

2 tablespoons clear honey

2 eggs

155 ml (5 fl oz/⅔ cup) whipping cream

220 g (7 oz) almond and honey nougat triangular-shaped chocolate bar, broken into pieces

TOPPING:

2 tablespoons clear honey

125 g (4 oz/1 cup) wheat and malted barley breakfast cereal

icing sugar for dusting, if desired

Preheat oven to 180C (350F/Gas 4). Grease and line a 22.5 cm (9 in) round, loose-bottomed cake tin. In a saucepan, melt butter, then stir in biscuit crumbs. Mix well, then press into base of cake tin.

In a bowl, beat cheese, honey and eggs until smooth. Bring cream to the boil in a small saucepan. Remove from the heat, add chocolate and stir until melted. Blend into cheese mixture. Turn into cake tin and bake in the oven for 30 minutes.

Meanwhile, make topping. Melt honey in a saucepan and stir in breakfast cereal. Spread over the cheesecake and return to the oven for a further 15 minutes. Leave to cool before removing from tin. Dust with icing sugar, if desired.

Serves 10–12.

—— CARDAMOM CHEESECAKE ——

1 quantity Chocolate Sponge Border, see page 11
90 g (3 oz/⅓ cup) butter
185 g (6 oz/1⅔ cups) semi-sweet biscuit crumbs
FILLING:
500 g (1 lb) medium fat soft cheese
315 ml (10 fl oz/1¼ cups) natural yogurt
3 eggs, separated
3 cardamom pods
90 g (3 oz/⅓ cup) caster sugar
finely grated peel and juice of 3 limes
4 teaspoons powdered gelatine
TO DECORATE:
3 limes, thinly sliced
155 ml (5 fl oz/⅔ cup) whipping cream

Cut sponge border to fit the inside of a 22.5 cm (9 in) loose-bottomed cake tin. Line base of tin with greaseproof paper. In a saucepan, melt butter, then stir in biscuit crumbs. Mix well, then press into base of cake tin.

In a bowl, beat cheese, yogurt and egg yolks until smooth. Split cardamom pods and put the seeds into a mortar with 3 teaspoons sugar and grind until smooth. Beat into cheese mixture with lime peel and juice.

Sprinkle gelatine over 3 tablespoons water in a small bowl and leave to soften for 2–3 minutes. Stand the bowl in a saucepan of hot water and stir until dissolved and quite hot. Stir into cheese mixture.

Whisk egg whites with remaining sugar until they form soft peaks, then fold into cheese mixture. Turn into cake tin and leave to set in the refrigerator for 2–3 hours.

To decorate, trim sponge border level with filling. Form lime slices into twists. Arrange around edge of cheesecake. Whip cream and pipe rosettes of cream into lime twists.

Serves 8–10.

GEORGE HANDLEY CHEESECAKE

90 g (3 oz/⅓ cup) butter
185 g (6 oz/1⅔ cups) ginger biscuit crumbs
FILLING:
500 g (1 lb) medium fat soft cheese
3 eggs
90 g (3 oz/⅓ cup) caster sugar
3 teaspoons plain flour
60 g (2 oz/⅓ cup) sultanas
TOPPING:
3 small oranges
470 ml (15 fl oz/1¾ cups) boiling water
60 g (2 oz/¼ cup) light muscovado sugar
2 tablespoons clear honey, plus extra for glazing
2 cloves
1 cinnamon stick
½ a bay leaf
5 whole allspice

Prepare oranges for topping. Cut into 0.3 cm (⅛ in) thick slices and put into a saucepan with boiling water, muscovado sugar, 2 table spoons honey and the spices. Cover and simmer for 20–25 minutes or until tender.

Meanwhile, preheat oven to 180C (350F/Gas 4). Grease and line a 20 cm (8 in) round, loose-bottomed cake tin. In a saucepan, melt butter, then stir in biscuit crumbs. Mix well, then press into base of cake tin.

To make filling, beat cheese, eggs, caster sugar and flour together in a bowl until smooth. Stir in sultanas. Turn into cake tin and bake in the oven for 45 minutes. Cool in tin.

To decorate, drain orange slices on a wire rack, then arrange on top of cheesecake, starting at edge of cake and overlapping in a spiral pattern into centre. Brush with a little extra honey for a shiny glaze.

Serves 8–10.

— SPICED HONEY CHEESECAKE —

1 quantity Sweet Shortcrust Pastry, see page 13

FILLING:

500 g (1 lb) low fat soft cheese

315 ml (10 fl oz/1¼ cups) natural yogurt

4 tablespoons clear honey

3 eggs

1 teaspoon ground cinnamon

¼ teaspoon ground allspice

pinch of ground cloves

TOPPING:

250 ml (8 fl oz/1 cup) orange juice

1 tablespoon clear honey

6 teaspoons cornflour

strips of orange peel

Preheat oven to 180C (350F/Gas 4). Grease a 20 cm (8 in) round, loose-bottomed cake tin. Roll out pastry on a lightly floured surface to a circle 25 cm (10 in) in diameter and 0.5 cm (¼ in) thick. Lift pastry onto rolling pin and into cake tin. Trim sides so that they reach 5 cm (2 in) up sides of tin. Leave in refrigerator while preparing filling.

In a bowl, beat cheese, yogurt, honey and eggs until smooth. Stir in cinnamon, allspice and cloves and spoon into pastry case. Bake in the oven for 45 minutes or until a skewer inserted into cake comes away clean.

To decorate, put orange juice and honey into a small saucepan and bring to the boil. Mix cornflour with 3 tablespoons water, stir into pan and simmer until thickened. Pour the topping over the cheesecake, leave to cool, then refrigerate until set. Arrange strips of orange peel on the top before serving.

Serves 6–8.

– BANANA & LIME CHEESECAKE –

90 g (3 oz/⅓ cup) butter
250 g (8 oz/2¼ cups) ginger biscuit crumbs
½ teaspoon ground mixed spice
FILLING:
500 g (1 lb) full fat soft cheese
90 g (3 oz/⅓ cup), plus 6 teaspoons light muscovado sugar
finely grated peel and juice of 2 limes
2 ripe bananas, sliced
2 eggs, separated
TOPPING:
3 bananas
2 tablespoons lemon juice
strips of lime peel

Preheat oven to 180C (350F/Gas 4). Grease and line a 22.5 cm (9 in) round, loose-bottomed cake tin. In a saucepan, melt butter, then stir in biscuit crumbs and mixed spice. Mix well, then press into base of tin.

In a bowl, beat cheese, 90 g (3 oz/⅓ cup) sugar, lime peel and juice, sliced bananas and egg yolks until smooth. In a separate bowl, whisk egg whites and remaining sugar until firm. Fold into cheese mixture with a large metal spoon, then turn into cake tin.

Bake in the oven for 1 hour. Leave to cool in the tin.

To decorate, slice bananas thinly and toss in lemon juice to prevent discoloration. Overlap banana slices over surface of cake. Chill, then decorate with lime peel to serve.

Serves 8–10.

CHEESE & CELERY CAKE

90 g (3 oz/⅓ cup) butter

250 g (8 oz/2¼ cups) semi-sweet biscuit crumbs

60 g (2 oz/½ cup) ground walnuts

FILLING:

500 g (1 lb) Ricotta cheese

125 ml (4 fl oz/½ cup) thick sour cream

2 eggs

3 teaspoons plain flour

salt and pepper

60 g (2 oz) sticks celery, chopped

90 g (3 oz/¾ cup) roughly chopped walnuts

TO DECORATE:

125 g (4 oz) sticks celery

6 walnut halves

Preheat oven to 180C (350F/Gas 4). Grease and line a 17.5 cm (7 in) round, spring-form cake tin. In a saucepan, melt butter, then stir in biscuit crumbs and ground walnuts. Mix well, then press into base of cake tin.

Put the cheese, sour cream and eggs into a blender or food processor and process until smooth. Add flour and season with salt and pepper. Stir in chopped celery and chopped walnuts. Turn into cake tin and bake in the oven for 50 minutes. Leave to cool before releasing the tin.

To decorate, cut celery into 6 cm (2½ in) strips and arrange in a fan shape around edge of cake. Arrange 6 walnut halves on the top. Serve as a starter or cheese course.

Serves 6–8.

— HERB & GARLIC BOMBE —

500 g (1 lb) cottage cheese
90 g (3 oz) full fat soft cheese
125 ml (4 fl oz/½ cup) thick sour cream
3 garlic cloves, crushed
2 tablespoons chopped fresh parsley
2 tablespoons chopped fresh thyme
pepper
TO FINISH:
5 tablespoons chopped fresh parsley
1 tomato rose

In a bowl, beat the cheeses and sour cream until smooth. Add garlic, parsley, thyme and pepper.

Line a semi-circular wire strainer or sieve with muslin. Fill with cheese mixture, place strainer or sieve over a bowl and leave to drain overnight.

Turn cheese out onto a board and roll in chopped parsley. Transfer to a serving plate and garnish with a tomato rose. Serve with cheese biscuits for a buffet party or as a cheese course with water biscuits.

Serves 6–8.

-HAM & MUSHROOM TERRINE-

30 g (1 oz) Parma ham

45 g (1½ oz/9 teaspoons) butter

1 small onion, chopped

3 teaspoons plain flour

125 ml (4 fl oz/½ cup) milk

2 egg yolks

black pepper

250 g (8 oz) Ricotta cheese

60 g (2 oz) cooked ham, chopped

60 g (2 oz) button mushrooms

TO GARNISH:

mushroom slices

sprig of parsley

Grease and line the base and long sides of a 22.5 cm (9 in) terrine. Line terrine with Parma ham.

In a saucepan, melt butter, add onion and cook until soft but not coloured. Stir in flour and cook for 1–2 minutes, then gradually add milk, stirring until thick. Stir in egg yolks, season with black pepper and leave mixture to cool.

Put sauce into a blender or food processor with cheese and process until smooth. Add chopped ham. Put mushrooms into a bowl and cover with boiling water. Leave for 2–3 minutes; drain. Stir into cheese mixture, then spoon into terrine. Chill in the refrigerator for 2 hours. Garnish the terrine with a few mushroom slices and a sprig of parsley before serving.

Serves 6–8.

Note: Serve the terrine with a green salad.

TURKEY CHEESECAKE

90 g (3 oz) packet stuffing mix
FILLING:
500 g (1 lb) Ricotta cheese
3 eggs
3 teaspoons plain flour
salt and pepper
30 g (1 oz/6 teaspoons) butter
1 onion, chopped
2 tablespoons chopped fresh chives
185 g (6 oz) cooked turkey, chopped
TOPPING:
185 g (6 oz) cranberries
125 ml (4 fl oz/½ cup) orange juice
3 teaspoons granulated sugar
6 teaspoons cornflour
6-8 holly leaves

Make up stuffing according to packet instructions. Press into base and up sides of a 20 cm (8 in) round, spring-form cake tin. Preheat oven to 180C (350F/Gas 4).

Put cheese, eggs, flour, salt and pepper into a blender or food processor and blend until smooth.

In a frying pan, melt butter, add onion and cook until soft but not coloured. Leave to cool, then add to cheese mixture. Stir in chives and turkey. Turn into cake tin and bake in the oven for 50 minutes.

To make topping, put cranberries in saucepan with orange juice and sugar. Bring to boil and simmer for about 5 minutes until berries pop.

Mix cornflour with 3 teaspoons water, stir into cranberries and simmer until thick. Spread cranberry topping over cooked cheesecake and leave to cool before releasing cake tin. Decorate with holly leaves, but remove them before serving.

Serves 6-8.

PARTY ROYALS

750 g (1½ lb) Jersey Royal or other new potatoes
125 g (4 oz) full fat soft cheese
125 ml (4 fl oz/½ cup) thick sour cream
2 tablespoons chopped fresh chives
juice of ½ a lemon
pinch of cayenne pepper
TO DECORATE:
60 g (2 oz) lumpfish roe
small bunch of chervil
1 lemon, cut into 24 tiny wedges

Cook potatoes in a saucepan of boiling salted water for 20 minutes or until tender. Rinse under cold water and set aside.

Put cheese and sour cream into a blender or food processor and blend until smooth. Stir in chives, lemon juice and cayenne pepper.

Cut tops off cooled potatoes and scoop out potato with a teaspoon. Fill the shell with cheese mixture and top with lumpfish roe.

Garnish each one with a sprig of chervil and a tiny wedge of lemon. Arrange in dark brown paper cases and chill before serving.

Makes 24.

— SMOKED TROUT TERRINE —

30 g (1 oz) aspic jelly crystals
1 lemon, thinly sliced
2 tomatoes, thinly sliced
sprigs of dill
FILLING:
375 g (12 oz) smoked trout
125 g (4 oz) medium fat curd cheese
60 g (2 oz/¼ cup) soft butter
juice of 1 lemon
pinch of cayenne pepper
pinch of ground mace
1 tablespoon chopped fresh parsley

Melt the aspic jelly crystals according to the packet instructions and leave to cool in a bowl set in a larger bowl of ice. Place a 20 cm (8 in) rectangular terrine in the freezer.

When aspic has cooled to consistency of pouring oil, coat inside of terrine. Place 6 slices of lemon in base of terrine. Arrange tomato slices in between lemon slices. Place sprigs of dill along sides of terrine.

Reserve remaining lemon, tomato and dill for garnishing.

Pour a second layer of aspic into terrine to coat base and sides – if aspic has started to set, place bowl over a saucepan of boiling water for a few seconds and stir until melted again. Chill in the refrigerator.

To make filling, discard trout bones and place flesh in a blender or food processor. Add cheese and butter and blend until smooth. Stir in lemon juice, cayenne pepper, mace and parsley. Turn into terrine and leave in the refrigerator for 1 hour or until firm.

To serve, stand terrine in a bowl of hot water for 15 seconds. Place a serving dish upside down over terrine, then invert dish and terrine to turn out. Garnish with reserved lemon, tomato and dill.

Serves 6–8.

——SWISS CHEESE RAMEQUINS——

1 quantity Sweet Shortcrust Pastry, see page 13

FILLING:

75 ml (2½ fl oz/⅓ cup) milk

75 ml (2½ fl oz/⅓ cup) whipping cream

2 teaspoons plain flour

1 egg

60 g (2 oz/½ cup) grated Gruyère cheese

30 g (1 oz/¼ cup) grated Parmesan cheese

3 teaspoons kirsch

pepper

pinch of grated nutmeg

TO GARNISH:

sprigs of parsley

Preheat oven to 220C (425F/Gas 7). Grease 12 small tartlet moulds. Roll out pastry on a lightly floured surface as thinly as possible. Cut out 12 circles with a fluted cutter 2.5 cm (1 in) larger in diameter than the moulds and line the moulds. Refrigerate while preparing filling.

Put milk and cream into a small mixing bowl. Sprinkle flour over surface and stir well with a fork. Beat in egg, cheeses and kirsch. Season with pepper and nutmeg.

Spoon mixture into pastry cases and bake near top of the oven for 12–15 minutes until risen. Garnish with sprigs of parsley and serve at once.

Makes 12.

Note: The pastry cases and cheese mixture can be prepared in advance and the mixture spooned into pastry cases just before baking.

— TARAMASALATA ROULADE —

30 g (1 oz/6 teaspoons) butter

250 g (8 oz) spinach, washed, drained and chopped

pinch of grated nutmeg

salt and pepper

3 teaspoons plain flour

2 tablespoons grated Parmesan cheese

3 eggs, separated

FILLING:

250 g (8 oz) Ricotta cheese

125 g (4 oz) taramasalata

TO GARNISH:

tomato slices

hard-boiled egg slices

sprig of parsley

Preheat oven to 200C (400F/Gas 6). Grease and line a 30 cm (12 in) square baking sheet.

In a saucepan, melt butter, then stir in spinach and cook for 3–4 minutes. Stir in nutmeg, salt and pepper to taste.

Mix flour and Parmesan cheese into egg yolks in a bowl, then stir into spinach. In a separate bowl, whisk egg whites until firm, then fold into spinach mixture with a metal spoon. Spread mixture onto baking sheet and bake near top of the oven for 12 minutes, cover with a clean tea towel and leave to cool completely.

In a bowl, blend Ricotta cheese and taramasalata until smooth. Spread the mixture over the cooked spinach and roll up evenly. Garnish the roulade with tomato slices, hard-boiled egg slices and a sprig of parsley. Serve cut into 2.5 cm (1 in) slices.

Serves 6.

Note: Serve as a light lunch dish with a mixed salad.

GOAT'S CHEESE CAKE

60 g (2 oz/¼ cup) butter

125 g (4 oz/¾ cup) bulgar wheat

30 g (1 oz/3 tablespoons) sunflower seeds

FILLING:

9 teaspoons white wine

90 g (3 oz/½ cup) sultanas

90 g (3 oz) goat's cheese

185 g (6 oz) cottage cheese

2 eggs

pinch of cayenne pepper

3 teaspoons powdered gelatine

155 ml (5 fl oz/⅔ cup) whipping cream

TOPPING:

185 g (6 oz) green grapes

Line a 20 cm (8 in) round, spring-form cake tin. In a small saucepan, melt butter, then stir in bulgar wheat and sunflower seeds. Mix well, then press into cake tin.

Put wine into a saucepan, add sultanas and simmer until wine has been absorbed. Put cheeses, eggs and cayenne pepper into a bowl and beat until light.

Sprinkle gelatine over 2 table-spoons water in a small bowl and leave to soften for 2–3 minutes. Stand the bowl in a saucepan of hot water and stir until dissolved and quite hot. Stir into cheese mixture.

In a separate bowl, loosely whip cream and fold into cheese mixture. Turn into cake tin and leave to set in the refrigerator for 2–3 hours.

To decorate, cut grapes in half and remove pips. Remove cheese-cake from tin and cover surface with grapes.

Serves 6.

TURKISH BOUREKAS

250 g (8 oz) filo pastry
185 g (6 oz/¾ cup) butter, melted
1 egg, beaten
30 g (1 oz/3 tablespoons) sesame seeds
30 g (1 oz/3 tablespoons) poppy seeds
FILLING:
375 g (12 oz) feta cheese
1 egg
15 g (½ oz/¼ cup) fresh breadcrumbs
3 tablespoons chopped fresh parsley
black pepper
4 small tomatoes, each cut into 6 slices
TO GARNISH:
tomato slices
sprig of parsley

Lightly grease a baking sheet. Prepare filling. Crumble feta cheese into a bowl, stir in egg, then add breadcrumbs and beat until smooth. Add parsley and season with black pepper.

Working with one sheet of filo pastry at a time, keeping the remainder covered with a damp cloth, cut lengthwise into 7.5 cm (3 in) wide strips. You should have 24 strips. Brush with butter. Preheat oven to 200C (400F/Gas 6).

Place a slice of tomato at one end, then put a spoonful of filling on top. Fold pastry over to form a triangle and continue folding until complete length has been folded. Repeat with remaining strips.

Place triangles on baking sheet. Brush with beaten egg. Sprinkle sesame seeds over half the triangles and poppy seeds over remainder. Bake in the oven for 25 minutes or until golden brown. Garnish the bourekas with tomato slices and a sprig of parsley.

Makes 24.

Variation: Cocktail bourekas can be made by reducing width of pastry strips to 5 cm (2 in).

—STRAWBERRY SMOOTH CAKE—

see page 48

— RASPBERRY CHEESECAKE —

see page 68

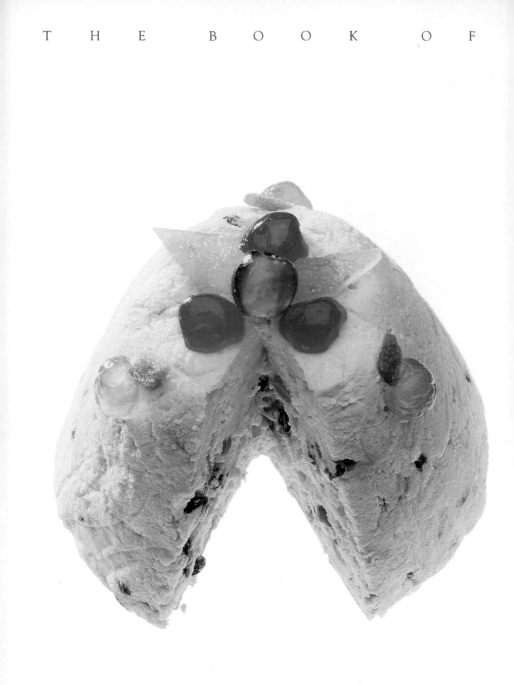

PASKHA

see page 20

—CHOC & ORANGE TERRINE—

see page 98

── SMOKED TROUT TERRINE ──

see page 109

— TARAMASALATA ROULADE —

see page·111

INDEX